STUDY GUIDE

for use with

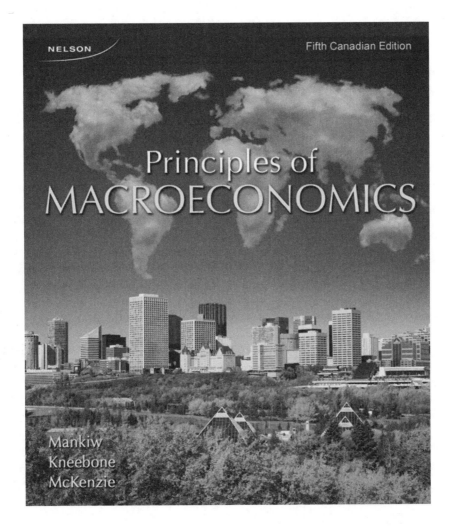

NELSON

Fifth Canadian Edition

Principles of
MACROECONOMICS

Mankiw
Kneebone
McKenzie

Prepared by PETER FORTURA
And SHAHRAM MANOUCHEHRI

NELSON EDUCATION

Principles of Macroeconomics

Fifth Canadian Edition

Study Guide

Mankiw,
Kneebone,
McKenzie,
Fortura

NELSON / EDUCATION

ISBN-13: 978-0-17-662295-4
ISBN-10: 0-17-662295-0

Consists of Selections from:

Principles of Macroeconomics Study Guide, Fifth Edition
Mankiw/Kneebone/McKenzie/Fortura/Manouchehri
ISBN 0-17-647135-9, © 2011

PREFACE

Economics is a way of thinking. It provides a tool kit for solving problems and making decisions. You may be tempted to learn economics by simply listening to lectures or relying on common sense. Do not be fooled. Economics cannot be learned by osmosis. Learning requires active participation by the student. This means solving problems and answering questions, then looking at the reasons behind both the correct and incorrect answers.

This *Study Guide* was written to accompany the fifth Canadian edition of *Principles of Macroeconomics*, by N. Gregory Mankiw, Ronald D. Kneebone, and Kenneth J. McKenzie. It was written with only one audience in mind—you, the student. It is intended to complement the material provided in the text and your instructor's lectures, thereby helping you to be successful in this course.

Objectives of the *Study Guide*

There are three broad objectives to the *Study Guide*. First, it reinforces the text and improves your understanding of the material presented in the text. Second, it provides you with experience in using economic theories and tools to solve actual economic problems— learning by doing! Third, the questions and problems allow you to validate areas of successful learning and to highlight areas needing additional study.

Organization of the *Study Guide*

Each chapter in the *Study Guide* corresponds to a chapter in the fifth Canadian edition of *Principles of Macroeconomics* text. Each *Study Guide* chapter includes the following sections:

I. *Chapter Overview:* This section begins with a description of the purpose of the chapter and of how the chapter fits into the overall framework of the text. The overview also includes helpful hints to guide the student's intuition in understanding the material.

II. *Self-Testing Challenges:* This section begins with true/false questions and multiple-choice questions. These questions provide useful feedback in preparation for an exam, particularly if the student analyzes the right and wrong answers. Next, there are short-answer questions and practice problems, which provide applications and important extensions of the material in the text. The practice problems are generally multiple-step problems, while each short-answer question is generally based on a single topic in the text. The section ends with an advanced critical thinking problem, which applies the economic reasoning and tools developed in the chapter to a real-world problem.

III. *Solutions:* This section provides answers to all of the questions and problems in the *Study Guide*. Explanations are provided for the false responses to the true/false questions.

Use of the *Study Guide*

A study guide is not a substitute for a text. Use this *Study Guide* in conjunction with the *Principles of Macroeconomics* text, not in place of it. How one best uses a study guide is largely a personal matter. Most students will prefer to read through the entire chapter in the text and then work through the *Study Guide*, identifying the areas which need further study and the areas which are already mastered.

Multiple-choice questions tend to be the most commonly used type of exam question. Yet students often encounter difficulties with this type of question because they find that many of the choices differ only slightly. Thus, students should develop and practise strategies for doing multiple-choice questions. The following are some helpful strategies: read each question and all of the choices very carefully—often, only one word is the difference between two of the choices. Eliminate any obviously wrong choices. Mark-up the page with notes, arrows, and diagrams. Remember that the correct answer may not be immediately evident— most questions will require you to analyze numerical and graphical information.

Acknowledgments

I would like to thank Gregory Mankiw for having written such an innovative and lively text, and the Canadian authors for carefully adapting Mankiw's ideas to fit the Canadian experience. Thanks also to David Hakes who wrote the *Principles of Macroeconomics Study Guide* for the U.S. market. His excellent work made producing the Canadian edition a truly enjoyable task. I also thank executive editor Craig Dyer and the development team at My Editor, for their support throughout the process.

Final Thoughts

Economics can be a tremendously exciting and enjoyable field of study. But it can also be intimidating. I hope that this *Study Guide* will improve your understanding of economics, so that you are able to enjoy the subject as much as I do.

Peter Fortura

CONTENTS

Part 1: Introduction

Chapter 1	Ten Principles of Economics	1
Chapter 2	Thinking Like an Economist	13
	Appendix: Graphing: A Brief Review	28
Chapter 3	Interdependence and the Gains from Trade	33

Part 2: Supply and Demand: How Markets Work

Chapter 4	The Market Forces of Supply and Demand	51

Part 3: The Data of Macroeconomics

Chapter 5	Measuring a Nation's Income	63
Chapter 6	Measuring the Cost of Living	77

Part 4: The Real Economy in the Long Run

Chapter 7	Production and Growth	91
Chapter 8	Saving, Investment, and the Financial System	103
Chapter 9	Unemployment and Its Natural Rate	117

Part 5: Money and Prices in the Long Run

Chapter 10	The Monetary System	129
Chapter 11	Money Growth and Inflation	141

Part 6: The Macroeconomics of Open Economies

Chapter 12	Open-Economy Macroeconomics: Basic Concepts	155
Chapter 13	A Macroeconomic Theory of the Open Economy	169

Part 7: Short-Run Economic Fluctuations

Chapter 14	Aggregate Demand and Aggregate Supply	183
Chapter 15	The Influence of Monetary and Fiscal Policy on Aggregate Demand	199
Chapter 16	The Short-Run Tradeoff between Inflation and Unemployment	213

Part 8: Final Thoughts

Chapter 17	Five Debates over Macroeconomic Policy	227

CHAPTER 1 Ten Principles of Economics

I. Chapter Overview

A. Context and Purpose

Chapter 1 is the first chapter in a three-chapter section that serves as the introduction to the text. Chapter 1 introduces ten fundamental principles on which the study of economics is based. In a broad sense, the rest of the text is an elaboration on these ten principles. Chapter 2 develops how economists approach problems, while Chapter 3 explains how individuals and countries gain from trade.

The purpose of Chapter 1 is to lay out ten economic principles that will serve as building blocks for the rest of the text. The ten principles can be grouped into three categories: how people make decisions, how people interact, and how the economy works as a whole. Throughout the text, references will repeatedly be made to these ten principles.

B. Helpful Hints

1. *Place yourself in the story.* Throughout the text, most economic situations will be composed of economic actors—buyers and sellers, borrowers and lenders, firms and workers, and so on. When you are asked to address how any economic actor would respond to economic incentives, place yourself in the story as the buyer or the seller, the borrower or the lender, the producer or the consumer. Do not think of yourself always as the buyer (a natural tendency) or always as the seller. You will find that your role playing will usually produce the right response once you learn to think like an economist—which is the topic of the next chapter.

2. *Trade is not a zero-sum game.* Some people see an exchange in terms of winners and losers. Their reaction to trade is that, after the sale, if the seller is happy, the buyer must be sad because the seller must have taken something from the buyer. That is, they view trade as a *zero-sum game* where what one gains the other must have lost. They fail to see that both parties to a voluntary transaction gain because each party is allowed to specialize in what it can produce most efficiently, and then trade for items that are produced more efficiently by others. Nobody loses, because trade is voluntary. Therefore, a government policy that limits trade reduces the potential gains from trade.

3. *An externality can be positive.* Because the classic example of an externality is pollution, it is easy to think of an externality as a cost that lands on a bystander. However, an externality can be positive in that it can be a benefit that lands on a bystander. For example, education is often cited as a product that emits a positive externality because when your neighbour educates herself, she is likely to be more reasonable, responsible, productive, and politically astute. In short, she is a better neighbour. Positive externalities, just as much as negative externalities, may be a reason for the government to intervene to promote efficiency.

II. Self-Testing Challenges

A. True/False Questions

_____1.   When the government redistributes income with taxes and welfare, the economy becomes more efficient.

_____2.   When economists say, "There is no such thing as a free lunch," they mean that all economic decisions involve tradeoffs.

_____3.   Adam Smith's "invisible hand" concept describes how corporate business reaches into the pockets of consumers like an "invisible hand."

_____4.   Rational people systematically and purposefully do the best they can to achieve their objectives.

_____5.   Canada will benefit economically if we eliminate trade with Asian countries because we will be forced to produce more of our own cars and clothes.

_____6.   When a jet flies overhead, the noise it generates is an externality.

_____7.   A tax on beer raises the price of beer and provides an incentive for consumers to drink more.

_____8.   An incentive is something that induces a person to act.

_____9.   Sue is better at cleaning and Bob is better at cooking. It will take fewer hours to eat and clean if Bob specializes in cooking and Sue specializes in cleaning than if they share the household duties evenly.

_____10.   High and persistent inflation is caused by moderate growth in the quantity of money in the economy.

_____11.   In the short run, a reduction in inflation tends to cause a reduction in unemployment.

_____12.   An auto manufacturer should continue to produce additional automobiles as long as the firm is profitable, even if the cost of the additional units exceeds the price received.

_____13. An individual farmer requires property rights to benefit from a market economy.

_____14. To a student, the opportunity cost of going to a basketball game would include the price of the ticket and the value of the time that could have been spent studying.

_____15. Workers in Canada have a relatively high standard of living because Canada has a relatively high minimum wage.

B. Multiple-Choice Questions

1. Which one of the following involve(s) a tradeoff faced by societies?
    a. buying a new car
    b. going to university
    c. watching a football game on Sunday afternoon
    d. guns and butter

2. Which one of the following is a reason that tradeoffs are required?
    a. because wants are unlimited and resources are efficient
    b. because wants are unlimited and resources are economical
    c. because wants are unlimited and resources are scarce
    d. because wants are unlimited and resources are unlimited

3. Which one of the following best defines what economics is the study of?
    a. how to avoid having to make tradeoffs
    b. how society manages its scarce resources
    c. how to fully satisfy our unlimited wants
    d. how to reduce our wants until we are satisfied

4. Which one of the following describes when a rational person will act?
    a. when the action is ethical
    b. when the action makes money for the person
    c. when the action produces marginal costs that exceed marginal benefits
    d. when the action produces marginal benefits that exceed marginal costs.

5. Which one of the following is an outcome of raising taxes and increasing welfare payments?
    a. improved equity at the expense of efficiency
    b. improved efficiency at the expense of equity
    c. reduced market power

6. Suppose Candace finds $20. If she chooses to use the $20 to go to a hockey game, which one of the following is her opportunity cost of going to the game?
   a. Nothing, because Candace found the money.
   b. $20 (because Candace could have used the $20 to buy other things).
   c. $20 (because Candace could have used the $20 to buy other things) plus the value of the time spent at the game.
   d. $20 (because Candace could have used the $20 to buy other things) plus the value of the time spent at the game, plus the cost of the dinner she consumed at the game.

7. Which one of the following best describes foreign trade?
   a. makes a country more equitable
   b. increases the scarcity of resources
   c. allows a country to avoid tradeoffs
   d. allows a country to have a greater variety of products at a lower cost than if it tried to produce everything at home

8. Because people respond to incentives, which one of the following would be expected to occur if the average salary of accountants increases by 50 percent while the average salary of teachers increases by 20 percent?
   a. Fewer students will attend university.
   b. Students will shift majors from education to accounting.
   c. Students will shift majors from accounting to education.

9. Which one of the following activities is **MOST** likely to produce an externality?
   a. A student reads a novel for pleasure.
   b. A student sits at home and watches television.
   c. A student has a party in her student residence room.
   d. A student eats a hamburger in the university cafeteria.

10. Which one of the following products would be **LEAST** capable of producing an externality?
    a. food
    b. cigarettes
    c. stereo equipment
    d. inoculations against disease

11. Which one of the following situations describes the **GREATEST** *market power*?
    a. Microsoft's impact on the price of desktop operating systems
    b. a farmer's impact on the price of corn
    c. Honda's impact on the price of autos
    d. a student's impact on university tuition

12. Which one of the following statements is true about a market economy?
    a. Taxes help prices communicate costs and benefits to producers and consumers.
    b. The strength of a market system is that it tends to distribute goods and services evenly across consumers.

    c.   Market participants act as if guided by an "invisible hand" to produce outcomes that maximize social welfare.

    d.   With a large enough computer, central planners could guide production more efficiently than markets could guide production.

13. Which one of the following is true according to Adam Smith's "invisible hand"?
    a.   Markets work even in the absence of property rights.
    b.   Many buyers and sellers acting independently and out of self-interest can promote general economic well-being without even realizing it.
    c.   Individuals who are concerned about the public good will almost invisibly promote increased social welfare.
    d.   Government plays a behind-the-scenes role in making a market economy work efficiently.

14. Which one of the following is a reason that workers in Canada enjoy a high standard of living?
    a.   because Canada has a high minimum wage
    b.   because unions in Canada keep the wage high
    c.   because workers in Canada are highly productive
    d.   because Canada has protected its industry from foreign competition

15. Which one of the following is a cause of high and persistent inflation?
    a.   unions increasing wages too much
    b.   OPEC raising the price of oil too much
    c.   regulations raising the cost of production too much
    d.   governments increasing the quantity of money too much

16. Which of the following statements occurs in the short run?
    a.   An increase in inflation temporarily increases unemployment.
    b.   A decrease in inflation temporarily increases unemployment.
    c.   Inflation and unemployment are unrelated in the short run.

17. Which one of the following could be inferred by an increase in the price of beef?
    a.   It tells consumers to buy more beef.
    b.   It tells consumers to buy less pork.
    c.   It tells producers to produce more beef.
    d.   It provides no information because prices in a market system are managed by planning boards.

18. Which one of the following is **NOT** part of the opportunity cost of going on vacation?
    1.   the money spent on food
    2.   the money spent on airplane tickets
    3.   the money spent on a Broadway show
    4.   the money that could have been earned by staying home and working

19. Which one of the following is a way that productivity can be increased?
    a.   by raising union wages
    b.   by raising minimum wage
    c.   by improving the education of workers

   d. by restricting trade with foreign countries

C. Short-Answer Questions

1. Is air scarce? Is clean air scarce? _____

_____

_____

2. What is the opportunity cost when an employee saves some of her paycheque?

_____

_____

3. Why is there a tradeoff between equity and efficiency? _____

_____

_____

4. Water is necessary for life. Diamonds are not. Is the marginal benefit of an additional glass of water greater or less than the marginal benefit of an additional one-carat diamond? Why? _____

_____

_____

5. Tom's car needs to be repaired. He has already paid $800 to have the transmission fixed, but it still does not work properly. Tom can sell the car "as is" for $2000. If the car was fixed, Tom could sell it for $2500. The car can be fixed, with a guarantee, for another $300. Should Tom repair his car? Why or why not? _____

_____

_____

6. Why have automotive air bags reduced deaths from auto crashes less than we had hoped? _____

_____

_____

7. Suppose one country is better at producing agricultural products (because it has more fertile land) while another country is better at producing manufactured goods (it has a better educational system and more engineers). If each country produced its specialty and traded, would there be more or less total output than if each country produced enough of its own agricultural and manufactured goods to meet its own needs? Why? _____

_____

_____

_____

8. In *The Wealth of Nations*, Adam Smith said, "It is not by the benevolence of the baker that you receive your bread." What did he mean? _____

_____

_____

9. If people save more and use it to build more physical capital, productivity will rise and people will have rising standards of living in the future. What is the opportunity cost of future growth?_____

_____

10. If the government printed twice as much money, what would happen to prices?_____

_____

_____

11. A goal for a society is to distribute resources equitably or fairly. How should resources be distributed if everyone were equally talented and worked equally hard? What if people had different talents and some people worked hard while others did not?_____

_____

_____

_____

_____

12. Why are property rights important to a market economy?_____

_____

_____

D. Practice Problems

1. People respond to incentives. Governments can alter incentives with public policy, and hence behaviour. However, sometimes public policy generates unintended consequences by producing results that were not anticipated. Describe one unintended consequence of each of the following public policies.

   a. To help the "working poor," the government raises the minimum wage to $25 per hour._____

   _____

   _____

   b. To help the homeless, the government places rent controls on apartments that restrict rent to $100 per month._____

   _____

   _____

   c. To limit the consumption of gasoline, the government raises the tax on gasoline by $2.00 per litre. _____

   _____

   _____

   d. To reduce the consumption of drugs, the government makes drugs illegal.

   _____

   _____

e. To raise the population of wolves, the government prohibits the killing of wolves._____

2. Opportunity cost is what is given up to get an item. Because there is no such thing as a free lunch, what would likely be given up to obtain each of the items listed below?

a. Susan can work full time or go to university. She chooses university._____

_____

_____

_____

b. Susan can work full time or go to university. She chooses work

_____

_____

_____

_____

c. Farmer Jones has 100 hectares of land. He can plant corn, which yields 100 tonnes per hectare, or he can plant beans, which yield 40 tonnes per hectare. He chooses to plant corn. _____

_____

_____

d. Farmer Jones has 100 hectares of land. He can plant corn, which yields 100 tonnes per hectare, or he can plant beans, which yield 40 tonnes per hectare. He chooses to plant beans._____

_____

_____

e. In (a) and (b) above, and (c) and (d) above, which is the opportunity cost of which—university for work or work for university? Corn for beans or beans for corn?_____

_____

_____

E. Advanced Critical Thinking

Suppose the university decides to lower the cost of parking on campus by reducing the price of a parking permit from $300 per semester to $50 per semester.

1. What would happen to the number of students desiring to park their cars on campus?_____

_____

_____

2. What would happen to the amount of time it would take to find a parking place?_____

_____

_____

3. Thinking in terms of opportunity cost, would the lower price of a parking sticker necessarily lower the true cost of parking? _____

_____

_____

4. Would the opportunity cost of parking be the same for students with no outside employment and students with jobs earning $15 per hour?_____

_____

_____

III. Solutions

A. True/False Questions

1. F; the economy becomes less efficient because it decreases the incentive to work hard.
2. T
3. F; the "invisible hand" refers to how markets guide self-interested people to create desirable social outcomes.
4. T
5. F; all countries gain from voluntary trade.
6. T
7. F; higher prices reduce the quantity demanded.
8. T
9. T
10. F; high inflation is caused by excessive monetary growth.
11. F; a reduction in inflation tends to raise unemployment.
12. F; a manufacturer should produce as long as the marginal benefit exceeds the marginal cost.
13. T
14. T
15. F; workers in Canada have a high standard of living because they are productive.

B.   Multiple-Choice Questions

1. d	5. a	9. c	13. b	17. c
2. c	6. c	10. a	14. c	18. a
3. b	7. d	11. a	15. d	19. c
4. d	8. b	12. c	16. b	

C. Short-Answer Questions

1.   No, no need to give up anything to get it. Yes, it is not possible to have an unlimited amount without giving up something to get it (pollution equipment on cars, etc.).

2.   The items she could have enjoyed had she spent it (current consumption).

3.   Taxes and welfare make people more equal but reduce incentives for hard work, thus lowering total output.

4.   The marginal benefit of another glass of water is generally lower because the water supply is so large that one more glass is of little value. The opposite is true for diamonds.

5.   Yes, because the marginal benefit of fixing the car is $2500 – $2000 = $500 and the marginal cost is $300. The original repair payment is not relevant.

6.   The cost of an accident was lowered. This changed incentives, therefore people drive faster and have more accidents.

7.   There would be more total output if the countries specialize and trade because each country is doing what it does most efficiently.

8.   The baker produces the best bread possible, not out of kindness, but because it is in his best interest to do so. Self-interest can maximize social welfare.

9.   The opportunity cost of future growth is the need to give up consumption today.

10.   Prices would roughly double.

11.   Fairness would require that everyone get an equal share. Fairness would require that people not get an equal share.

12.   A farmer will not grow food if he expects his crop to be stolen. People rely on government to enforce their rights over the things they produce.

D. Practice Problems

1. a. Many would want to work at $25 per hour but few firms would want to hire low-productivity workers at this wage; therefore, it would create unemployment.

   b. Many renters would want to rent an apartment at $100 per month, but few landlords could produce an apartment at this price; therefore, this rent control would create more homelessness.

   c. Higher gas prices would reduce the number of kilometres driven. This would lower auto accidents, put less wear and tear on roads and cars, and reduce the demand for both cars and road repairs.

   d. This raises the price of drugs and makes selling them more profitable. This creates more drug sellers and increases violence as they fight to protect their turf.

   e. Restrictions on killing wolves reduce the population of animals upon which wolves may feed—e.g., rabbits, deer, etc.

2. a. She gives up income from work (and must pay tuition).

   b. She gives up a university degree and the increase in income throughout life that it would have brought her (but she does not have to pay tuition).

   c. He gives up 4000 tonnes of beans.

   d. He gives up 10 000 tonnes of corn.

   e. Each is the opportunity cost of the other because each decision requires giving something up.

E. Advanced Critical Thinking

1. More students would wish to park on campus.

2. It would take much longer to find a parking place.

3. No, because the value of the time spent looking for a parking place would have to be factored in.

4. No. Students who could be earning money working are giving up more while looking for a parking place than those with no outside employment. Therefore, their opportunity cost is higher.

If Japan specializes in television production, produces 3 televisions, and exports 1 television for 3 units of steel, Japan will be able to consume 2 televisions and 3 units of steel. When this point (2 televisions and 3 units of steel) is plotted on Japan's graph, it lies outside its production possibilities frontier. If Korea specializes, produces 8 units of steel, and exports 3 units for one television, Korea will be able to consume 5 units of steel and 1 television. When this point (5 units of steel and one television) is plotted on Korea's graph, it also lies outside its production possibilities frontier.

This is the gain from trade. Trade allows countries (and people) to specialize. Specialization increases world output. After trading, countries consume outside their individual production possibilities frontiers. In this way, trade is like an improvement in technology. It allows countries to move beyond their current production possibilities frontiers.

3. *Only comparative advantage matters—absolute advantage is irrelevant.* In the previous example, Japan had an absolute advantage in the production of televisions because it could produce 3 per hour while Korea could produce only 2. Korea had an absolute advantage in the production of steel because it could produce 8 units per hour compared to 6 for Japan.

To demonstrate that comparative advantage, not absolute advantage, determines specialization and trade, the previous example is altered such that Japan has an absolute advantage in the production of both goods. To this end, suppose Japan becomes twice as productive as in the previous table. That is, a worker can now produce 12 units of steel or 6 televisions per hour.

	Output	
	Steel (units/h)	Televisions (no./h)
Japan	12	6
Korea	8	2

Now Japan has an absolute advantage in the production of both goods. Japan's new production possibilities frontier is the dashed line in the previous graph. Will this change the analysis? Not at all. The opportunity cost of each good within Japan is the same—2 units of steel per television or one-half of a television per unit of steel (and Korea is unaffected). For this reason, Japan still has the identical comparative advantage as before and it will specialize in television production while Korea will specialize in steel. However, because productivity has doubled in Japan, its entire set of choices has improved and, thus, its material welfare has improved.

II. Self-Testing Challenges

A. True/False Questions

_____1.   If Japan has an absolute advantage in the production of an item, it must also have a comparative advantage in the production of that item.

_____2.   Comparative advantage, not absolute advantage, determines the decision to specialize in production.

_____3.   Absolute advantage is a comparison based on productivity.

_____4.   Self-sufficiency is the best way to increase one's material welfare.

_____5.   Comparative advantage is a comparison based on opportunity cost.

_____6.   If a producer is self-sufficient, the production possibilities frontier is also the consumption possibilities frontier.

_____7.   If a country's workers can produce five hamburgers per hour or ten bags of French fries per hour, absent trade, the price of one bag of fries is two hamburgers.

_____8.   If producers have different opportunity costs of production, trade will allow them to consume outside their production possibilities frontiers.

_____9.   If trade benefits one country, its trading partner must be worse off due to trade.

_____10. Talented people who are the best at everything have a comparative advantage in the production of everything.

_____11. The gains from trade can be measured by the increase in total production and consumption that comes from specialization.

_____12. When a country removes a specific import restriction, it always benefits every worker in that country.

_____13. If Germany's productivity doubles for everything it produces, this will not alter its prior pattern of specialization because it has not altered its comparative advantage.

_____14. If an advanced country has an absolute advantage in the production of everything, it will benefit if it eliminates trade with less developed countries and becomes completely self-sufficient.

_____15. If gains from trade are based solely on comparative advantage, and if all countries have the same opportunity costs of production, then there are no gains from trade

B. Multiple Choice Questions

1. Which one of the following situations is most likely for a nation that has an **absolute** advantage in the production of a good?
    a. It can benefit by restricting imports of that good.
    b. It will specialize in the production of that good and export it.
    c. It can produce that good using fewer resources than its trading partner.
    d. It can produce that good at a lower opportunity cost than its trading partner.

2. Which one of the following situations is most likely for a nation has a **comparative** advantage in the production of a good?
    a. It can benefit by restricting imports of that good.
    b. It must be the only country with the ability to produce that good.
    c. It can produce that good at a lower opportunity cost than its trading partner.
    d. It can produce that good using fewer resources than its trading partner.

3. Which one of the following statements about trade is true?
    a. People who are skilled at all activities cannot benefit from trade.
    b. Unrestricted international trade benefits every person in a country equally.
    c. Trade can benefit everyone in society because it allows people to specialize in activities in which they have an absolute advantage.
    d. Trade can benefit everyone in society because it allows people to specialize in activities in which they have a comparative advantage.

4. Which one of the following does the principle of comparative advantage state?
    a. Countries with a comparative advantage in the production of every good need not specialize.
    b. Countries should specialize in the production of goods that they enjoy consuming more than other countries enjoy consuming them.
    c. Countries should specialize in the production of goods for which they use fewer resources in production than do their trading partners.
    d. Countries should specialize in the production of goods for which they have a lower opportunity cost of production than do their trading partners.

5. Which one of the following statements is true?
    a. Self-sufficiency is the road to prosperity for most countries.
    b. A self-sufficient country consumes outside its production possibilities frontier.
    c. A self-sufficient country can, at best, consume on its production possibilities frontier.
    d. Only countries with an absolute advantage in the production of every good should strive to be self-sufficient.

6. Suppose a country's workers can produce 4 watches per hour or 12 rings per hour. Which one of the following is the domestic price of 1 ring if there is no trade?
    a. The domestic price of 1 ring is one-third of a watch.
    b. The domestic price of 1 ring is 3 watches.
    c. The domestic price of 1 ring is 4 watches.
    d. The domestic price of 1 ring is one-quarter of a watch.

7. Suppose a country's workers can produce 4 watches per hour or 12 rings per hour. Which one of the following is the opportunity cost of 1 watch if there is no trade?
    a. The opportunity cost of 1 watch is 3 rings.
    b. The opportunity cost of 1 watch is one-third of a ring.
    c. The opportunity cost of 1 watch is 4 rings.
    d. The opportunity cost of 1 watch is one-quarter of a ring.

The following table shows production data for Australia and Korea. Use this table for questions 8–15.

	Output	
	Food (no. units/worker/month)	Electronics (no. units/worker/month)
Australia	20	5
Korea	8	4

8. From the production data, which one of the following statements can be made about absolute advantage??
    a. Korea has an absolute advantage in the production of both food and electronics.
    b. Australia has an absolute advantage in the production of both food and electronics.
    c. Australia has an absolute advantage in the production of food while Korea has an absolute advantage in the production of electronics.
    d. Korea has an absolute advantage in the production of food while Australia has an absolute advantage in the production of electronics.

9. Which one of the following is the opportunity cost of 1 unit of electronics in Australia?
    a. 5 units of food
    b. one-fifth of a unit of food
    c. 4 units of food
    d. one-quarter of a unit of food

10. Which one of the following is the opportunity cost of 1 unit of electronics in Korea?
    a. 2 units of food
    b. one-half of a unit of food
    c. 4 units of food
    d. one-quarter of a unit of food

11. Which one of the following is the opportunity cost of 1 unit of food in Australia?
    a. 5 units of electronics
    b. one-fifth of a unit of electronics
    c. 4 units of electronics
    d. one-quarter of a unit of electronics

12. Which one of the following is the opportunity cost of 1 unit of food in Korea?
    a. 2 units of electronics
    b. one-half of a unit of electronics
    c. 4 units of electronics
    d. one-quarter of a unit of electronics

13. Which one of the following statements can be made about comparative advantage?
    a. Australia has a comparative advantage in the production of food while Korea has a comparative advantage in the production of electronics.
    b. Korea has a comparative advantage in the production of food while Australia has a comparative advantage in the production of electronics.
    c. Australia has a comparative advantage in the production of both food and electronics.
    d. Korea has a comparative advantage in the production of both food and electronics.

14. Which recommendation below would be the best for Korea?
    a. specialize in food production, export food, and import electronics
    b. specialize in electronics production, export electronics, and import food
    c. produce both goods because neither country has a comparative advantage
    d. produce neither good because it has an absolute disadvantage in the production of both goods

15. Prices of electronics can be stated in terms of units of food. Which one of the following is the range of prices of electronics for which both countries could gain from trade?
    a. The price must be greater than 4 units of food but less than 5 units of food.
    b. The price must be greater than 2 units of food but less than 4 units of food.
    c. The price must be greater than one-quarter of a unit of food but less than one-half of a unit of food.
    d. The price must be greater than one-fifth of a unit of food but less than one-quarter of a unit of food.

16.   Suppose the world consists of two countries—the United States and Canada. Further, suppose there are only two goods—food and clothing. Which one of the following statements best represents the situation?
   a. If the United States has an absolute advantage in the production of food, then Canada must have an absolute advantage in the production of clothing.
   b. If the United States has a comparative advantage in the production of food, Canada might also have a comparative advantage in the production of food.
   c. If the United States has a comparative advantage in the production of food, it must also have a comparative advantage in the production of clothing.
   d. If the United States has a comparative advantage in the production of food, then Canada must have a comparative advantage in the production of clothing.

Use the following production possibilities frontiers to answer questions 17–19. Assume each country has 20 workers and that each axis is measured in tonnes per month.

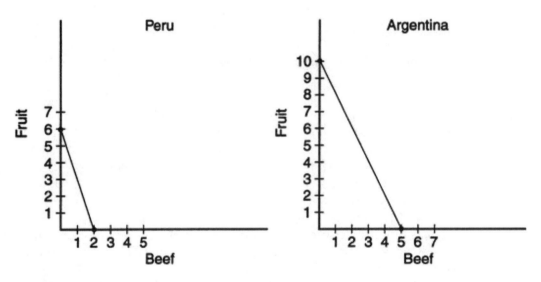

17. For which one of the following does Argentina have a comparative advantage in production?
   a. fruit
   b. beef
   c. both fruit and beef
   d. neither fruit nor beef

18. Which one of the following will Peru export?
   a. beef
   b. fruit
   c. both fruit and beef
   d. neither fruit nor beef

19. Which one of the following is the opportunity cost of producing a tonne of beef in Peru?
    a. one-third of a tonne of fruit
    b. 1 tonne of fruit
    c. 2 tonnes of fruit
    d. 3 tonnes of fruit

20. Joe is a tax accountant. He receives $100 per hour for preparing tax returns. He can type 5000 characters per hour into spreadsheets. He can hire an assistant who types 2500 characters per hour into spreadsheets. Which one of the following statements is the best recommendation?
    a. Joe should not hire an assistant because the assistant cannot type as fast as he can.
    b. Joe should hire the assistant as long as he pays the assistant less than $100 per hour.
    c. Joe should hire the assistant as long as he pays the assistant less than $50 per hour.

C. Short-Answer Questions

1. Why do people choose to become interdependent as opposed to self-sufficient?_____

_____

_____

2. Why is comparative advantage instead of absolute advantage important in determining trade?_____

_____

3. What are the gains from trade? _____

_____

_____

4. Why is a restriction of trade likely to reduce economic welfare?_____

_____

_____

5. Suppose that a lawyer earning $200 per hour can also type at 200 words per minute. Should the lawyer hire a secretary who can type only 50 words per minute? Why or why not?_____

_____

_____

6. Evaluate this statement: A technologically advanced country, which is better than its neighbour at producing everything, would be better off if it closed its borders to trade because the less productive country is a burden to the advanced country.

_____

_____

_____

D. Practice Problems

1. Angela is a college student. She takes a full load of classes and has only 5 hours per week for her hobby. Angela is artistic and can make 2 clay pots per hour or 4 coffee mugs per hour.

    a. Draw Angela's production possibilities frontier for pots and mugs based on the amount produced per week.

    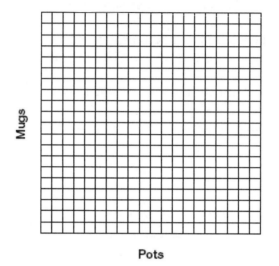

    Mugs (vertical axis)

    Pots (horizontal axis)

    b. What is Angela's opportunity cost of 1 pot? 10 pots? _____

    _____

    c. What is Angela's opportunity cost of 1 mug? 10 mugs?_____

    _____

    d. Why is her production possibilities frontier a straight line instead of bowed out like those presented in Chapter 2? _____

    _____

2. Suppose a worker in Germany can produce 15 computers or 5 tonnes of grain per month. Suppose a worker in Poland can produce 4 computers or 4 tonnes of grain per month. For simplicity, assume that each country has only one worker.

    a. Fill out the following table:

    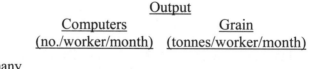

	Output	
	Computers (no./worker/month)	Grain (tonnes/worker/month)
Germany		
Poland		

b.   Graph the production possibilities frontier for each country.

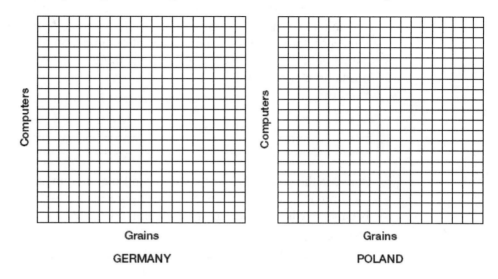

GERMANY   POLAND

c.   What is the opportunity cost of 1 computer in Germany? What is the opportunity cost of 1 tonne of grain in Germany?_____

_____

d.   What is the opportunity cost of 1 computer in Poland? What is the opportunity cost of 1 tonne of grain in Poland?_____

_____

e.   Which country has the absolute advantage in producing computers? Grain?_____

_____

f.   Which country has the comparative advantage in producing computers? Grain?_____

_____
_____
_____

g.   Each country should tend toward specialization in the production of which good? Why?_____

_____
_____
_____

h.   What are the range of prices for computers and grain for which both countries would benefit?_____

_____
_____

i.   Suppose Germany and Poland settle on a price of 2 computers for 1 tonne of grain or 0.5 tonnes of grain for a computer. Suppose each country specializes completely in production and they trade four computers for 2 tonnes of grain. Plot the final consumption points on the graphs made in part (b) above. Are these countries consuming inside or outside of their production possibilities frontier?_____

_____

_____

_____

j.   Suppose the productivity of a worker in Poland doubles so that a worker can produce 8 computers or 8 tonnes of grain per month. Which country has the absolute advantage in producing computers? Grain?_____

_____

_____

_____

k.   After the doubling of productivity in Poland, which country has a comparative advantage in producing computers? Grain? Has the comparative advantage changed? Has the economic welfare of either country changed?_____

_____

_____

_____

_____

l.   How would the analysis change if it was assumed, more realistically, that each country had 10 million workers?_____

_____

_____

_____

3.   Suppose a worker in Canada can produce 4 cars or 20 computers per month while a worker in Russia can produce 1 car or 5 computers per month. Again, for simplicity, assume each country has only one worker.

a.   Fill out the following table:

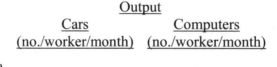

	Output	
	Cars (no./worker/month)	Computers (no./worker/month)
Canada		
Russia		

b.   Which country has the absolute advantage in the production of cars? Computers?_____

_____

_____

c. Which country has the comparative advantage in the production of cars? Computers?

_____

_____

_____

d. Are there any gains to be made from trade? Why or why not?_____

_____

_____

e. Does the answer in (d) above help pinpoint a source for gains from trade?_____

_____

_____

f. What might make two countries have different opportunity costs of production? (Use your imagination. This was not directly discussed in Chapter 3.)_____

_____

_____

_____

E. Advanced Critical Thinking

In an election debate a candidate says, "We need to stop the flow of foreign automobiles into our country. If we limit the importation of automobiles, our domestic auto production will rise and Canada will be better off."

1. Is it likely that Canada will be better off if it limits auto imports? Explain._____

_____

_____

2. Will anyone in Canada be better off if it limits auto imports? Explain._____

_____

_____

_____

3. In the real world, does every person in the country gain when restrictions on imports are reduced? Explain._____

_____

_____

_____

III. Solutions

A. True/False Questions

1.   F; absolute advantage compares the quantities of inputs used in production while comparative advantage compares the opportunity costs.
2. T
3. T
4. F; restricting trade eliminates gains from trade.
5. T
6. T
7. F; the price of 1 bag of fries is one-half of a hamburger.
8. T
9. F; voluntary trade benefits both traders.
10. F; a low opportunity cost of producing one good implies a high opportunity cost of producing the other good.
11. T
12. F; it may harm those involved in that industry.
13. T
14. F; voluntary trade benefits all traders.
15. T

B. Multiple-Choice Questions

1. c	6. a	11. d	16. d
2. c	7. a	12. b	17. b
3. d	8. b	13. a	18. b
4. d	9. c	14. b	19. d
5. c	10. a	15. b	20. c

C. Short-Answer Questions

1. Because a consumer gets a greater variety of goods at a much lower cost than he or she could produce by himself or herself. That is, there are gains from trade.

2. What is important in trade is how a country's costs without trade differ from another country's costs. This is determined by the relative opportunity costs across countries.

3. The additional output and consumption that comes from countries with different opportunity costs of production specializing in the production of the item for which they have the lower domestic opportunity cost.

4. Because it forces people to produce at a higher cost than they would pay when they trade.

5. Yes, as long as the secretary earns less than $50 per hour, the lawyer is ahead.

6. This is not true. All countries can gain from trade if their opportunity costs of production differ. Even the least productive country will have a comparative advantage at producing something, and it can trade this good to the advanced country for less than the advanced country's opportunity cost.

D. Practice Problems

1. a.

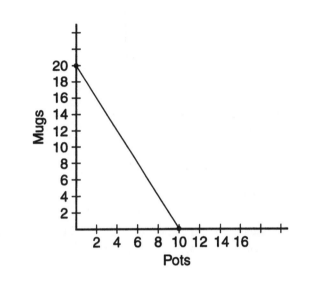

b. 2 mugs. 20 mugs.

c. One-half of a pot. 5 pots.

d. Because her resources can be moved from the production of one good to another at a constant rate.

2. a.

	Output	
	Computers (no./worker/month)	Grain (no./worker/month)
Germany	15	5
Poland	4	4

b.

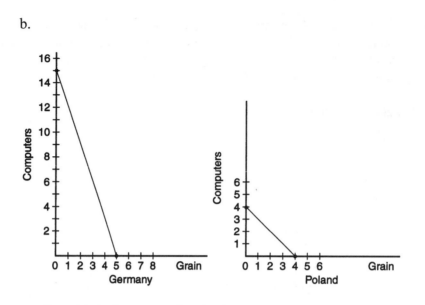

c. One-third of a tonne of grain. 3 computers.

d. 1 tonne of grain. 1 computer.

e. Germany because 1 worker can produce 15 compared to 4. Germany because 1 worker can produce 5 compared to 4.

f. Germany because a computer has the opportunity cost of only one-third of a tonne of grain compared to 1 tonne of grain in Poland. Poland because 1 tonne of grain has the opportunity cost of only 1 computer compared to 3 computers in Germany.

g. Germany should produce computers while Poland should produce grain because the opportunity cost of computers is lower in Germany and the opportunity cost of grain is lower in Poland. That is, each has a comparative advantage in those goods.

h. Grain must cost less than 3 computers to Germany. Computers must cost less than 1 tonne of grain to Poland.

7. If nominal GDP in 2010 exceeds nominal GDP in 2009, which one of the following must have occurred in production of real output?
   a. It must have risen.
   b. It must have fallen.
   c. It must have stayed the same.
   d. It must have risen or fallen because there is not enough information to determine what happened to real output.

8. Suppose a cobbler buys leather for $100 and thread for $50 and uses them to produce and sell $500 worth of shoes to consumers. Which one of the following is the contribution to GDP?
   a. $50
   b. $100
   c. $150
   d. $500

9. Which one of the following would be included in GDP?
   a. housework
   b. illegal drug sales
   c. intermediate sales
   d. legal services

10. Real GDP is measured in _____ prices, while nominal GDP is measured in _____ prices.
    a. domestic, foreign
    b. intermediate, final
    c. base year, current year
    d. current year, base year

The following table contains information about an economy that produces only pens and books. The base year is 2008. Use this information for questions 11–16.

Year	Price of Pens	Quantity of Pens	Price of Books	Quantity of Books
2008	$3	100	$10	50
2009	$3	120	$12	70
2010	$4	120	$14	70

11. Which one of the following is the value of nominal GDP for 2009?
    a. $800
    b. $1060
    c. $1200
    d. $1460

12. Which one of the following is the value of real GDP for 2009?
    a. $800
    b. $1060
    c. $1200
    d. $1460

13. Which one of the following is the value of the GDP deflator in 2009?
    a. 100
    b. 113
    c. 116
    d. 119

14. Which one of the following is the percentage increase in prices from 2008 to 2009?
    a. 0 percent
    b. 13 percent
    c. 16 percent
    d. 19 percent

15. Which one of the following is the approximate percentage increase in prices from 2009 to 2010?
    a. 0 percent
    b. 13 percent
    c. 16 percent
    d. 22 percent

16. Which one of the following is the percentage increase in real GDP from 2009 to 2010?
    a. 0 percent
    b. 7 percent
    c. 22 percent
    d. 27 percent

17. Which one of the following is **NOT** included in GDP?
    a. volunteer work
    b. medical services
    c. haircuts

18. Which one of the following is **NOT** included in Canadian GDP?
    a. grapes purchased by a Niagara winery
    b. legal services purchased by a homebuyer
    c. lawn care services purchased by a homeowner
    d. a new bridge purchased by the province of Prince Edward Island

19. Suppose Jane purchases a $60 000 BMW that was produced in Germany. Which one of the following describes how this would be recorded in the Canadian GDP accounts?
    a. Net exports increase by $60 000.
    b. Net exports decrease by $60 000.
    c. Investment increases by $60 000 and net exports increase by $60 000.
    d. Consumption increases by $60 000 and net exports decrease by $60 000.

20.   Which one of the following would be affected when a person purchases a new home?
      a.   investment
      b.   net exports
      c.   consumption
      d.   government purchases

C. Short-Answer Questions

1.   Why does income = expenditure = GDP? _____
       _____

2.   Define GDP and explain the important terms in the definition.
       _____
       _____
       _____
       _____
       _____

3.   What are the components of expenditure? Provide an example of each.
       _____
       _____
       _____

4.   Provide an example of a transfer payment. Is it included in GDP? Why or why not? _____
       _____
       _____

5.   If nominal GDP in 2010 exceeds nominal GDP in 2009, did real output rise? Did prices rise?_____
       _____

6.   If real GDP in 2010 exceeds real GDP in 2009, did real output rise? Did prices rise?_____
       _____
       _____
       _____

7.   If a Canadian buys a $35 000 Toyota that was fully produced in Japan, does this affect Canadian GDP? Show how this transaction would affect the appropriate expenditure categories that make up GDP._____
       _____
       _____
       _____

8.   In the year 2008, what was the approximate value of GDP per person? What component of GDP is the largest? _____
       _____
       _____

9.   Which contributes more when measuring GDP, a new diamond necklace purchased by a wealthy person or a soft drink purchased by a thirsty person? Why?_____

_____

_____

10.   If Serena hires someone to mow her lawn instead of doing it herself, what will happen to GDP? Why? Did output change?_____

_____

_____

D. Practice Problems

1.   a. Complete the following table. The data are in millions of dollars.

	Year 1	Year 2	Year 3
Gross domestic product	4532	4804	
Consumption		3320	3544
Investment	589	629	673
Government purchases	861		977
Net exports	−45	−58	−54

b. What is the largest expenditure component of GDP?_____

_____

_____

c. Does investment include the purchase of stocks and bonds? Why or why not?

_____

_____

_____

_____

d. Does the government purchases component include government spending on Employment Insurance benefits? Why or why not?

_____

_____

e. What does it mean when it is said that net exports are negative?

_____

_____

2. Suppose the base year in the following table is 2008.

Year	Production of X	Price per unit of X
2008	20 units	$5
2009	20 units	$10
2010	20 units	$20

a. What is nominal GDP for 2008, 2009, and 2010?_____

_____

b. What is real GDP for 2008, 2009, and
   2010?_____

_____

3. Suppose the following table records the total output and prices for an entire economy. Further, suppose the base year in the following table is 2009.

Year	Price of soft drink	Quantity of soft drink	Price of jeans	Quantity of jeans
2009	$1.00	200	$10.00	50
2010	$1.00	220	$11.00	50

a. What is the value of nominal GDP in 2009?_____

b. What is the value of real GDP in 2009?_____

c. What is the value of nominal GDP in 2010?_____

d. What is the value of real GDP in 2010?_____

e. What is the value of the GDP deflator in 2009?_____

f. What is the value of the GDP deflator in 2010?_____

g. From 2009 to 2010, prices rose approximately what percentage?_____

h. Was the increase in nominal GDP from 2009 to 2010 mostly due to an increase in real output or due to an increase in prices?_____

_____

_____

4.   Complete the following table.

Year	Nominal GDP	Real GDP	GDP deflator
1		$100	100
2	$120		120
3	$150	$125	

a.   What year is the base year? Explain why?_____

_____

_____

b.   From year 1 to year 2, did real output rise or did prices rise? Explain.

_____

_____

c.   From year 2 to year 3, did real output rise or did prices rise? Explain.

_____

_____

E. Advanced Critical Thinking

Sean is watching a news report with his father. The news anchor points out that a certain troubled Caribbean nation generates a GDP per person of only CDN$4800 per year. Because Sean's father knows GDP in Canada is approximately CDN$48 000 per person, he suggests that Canadians are materially 10 times better off in Canada than in the Caribbean nation.

1.   Is the father's statement accurate?_____

2.   What general category of production is not captured by GDP in both Canada and the Caribbean nation?_____

_____

3.   Provide some examples of this type of activity._____

_____

_____

4.   Why would the exclusion of this type of production affect the measurement of Caribbean output more than Canadian output?_____

_____

_____

5.   Does this mean that residents of the Caribbean nation are actually as well off materially as residents in Canada?_____

_____

_____

_____

III. Solutions

A. True/False Questions

1.   T
2.   F; contribution is based on market value.
3.   F; the garage is the final good, valued at $5000.
4.   T
5.   F; prices or real output could have risen.
6.   T
7.   F; transfer payments are expenditures for which no good or service is received in return.
8.   F; consumption is the largest component of GDP.
9.   T
10.   F; goods are counted in the year produced.
11.   T
12.   T
13.   T
14.   T
15.   F; NX = X – M.

B. Multiple-Choice Questions

1. a	5. d	9. d	13. b	17. a
2. d	6. a	10. c	14. b	18. a
3. c	7. d	11. c	15. d	19. d
4. c	8. d	12. b	16. a	20. a

C. Short-Answer Questions

1.   Because the income of the seller equals the expenditure of the buyer and GDP can be measured with either one.

2.   Market value of all final goods and services produced within a country in a given period of time. "Market value" – price paid, "of all" – all legal production, "final" – to end users, "goods and services" – includes services, "produced" – no used items, "within a country" – inside borders, "in a given period" – per quarter or year.

3.   Consumption (food), investment (factory), government purchases (military equipment), net exports (sale of wheat to Japan minus purchase of wine from Germany).

4.   Social assistance payments. No, because the government received no good or service in return.

5.   It is not certain which rose, prices or real output, because an increase in either prices or real output will cause nominal output to rise.

6. Real output rose because the value of output in each year is measured in constant base year prices. There is no information on prices.

7. No. Consumption would increase by $35 000 and net exports would decrease by $35 000. As a result, Canadian GDP is unaffected.

8. GDP per person, or the amount of expenditure for the average Canadian, was about $48 000 per year. Consumption made up about 56 percent of GDP, or about $26 735 per person.

9. A diamond necklace because GDP measures market value.

10. GDP will rise because the mowing of the lawn now becomes a market transaction. However, output did not really rise.

D. Practice Problems

1. a.

	Year 1	Year 2	Year 3
Gross domestic product	4532	4804	5140
Consumption	3127	3320	3544
Investment	589	629	673
Government purchases	861	913	977
Net exports	−45	−58	−54

b. Consumption

c. No, because that transaction is a purchase of a financial asset, not a purchase of currently produced capital goods.

d. No, because Employment Insurance benefits are expenditures for which the government receives no production in return.

e. It means that imports exceed exports.

2. a. $100, $200, $400.

b. $100, $100, $100.

3. a. $700.

    b. $700.

    c. $770.

    d. $720.

    e. 100.

    f. 107.

    g. $(107 - 100)/100 = 0.07 = 7\%$.

    h. Percent increase in nominal GDP $(\$770 - \$700)/700 = 0.10 = 10\%$. Percent increase in prices = 7%, therefore, most of the increase was due to prices.

4.

Year	Nominal GDP	Real GDP	GDP deflator
1	$100	$100	100
2	$120	$100	120
3	$150	$125	120

    a. Year 1, because the GDP deflator = 100.

    b. Prices rose 20 percent and real output stayed the same.

    c. Prices stayed the same and real output rose 25 percent.

E. Advanced Critical Thinking

1. No.

2. Nonmarket activities.

3. Household production done by an individual without pay, such as gardening, cleaning, sewing, home improvement or construction, child supervision, etc.

4. A greater proportion of the output produced by lesser developed nations is nonmarket output. That is, it is not sold and recorded as a market transaction.

5. No. It just means that quantitative comparisons between nations of greatly different levels of development are very difficult and often inaccurate.

CHAPTER 6   Measuring the Cost of Living

I. Chapter Overview

A. Context and Purpose

Chapter 6 is the second chapter of a two-chapter sequence that deals with how economists measure output and prices in the macroeconomy. Chapter 5 addressed how economists measure output. Chapter 6 develops how economists measure the overall price level in the macroeconomy.

The purpose of Chapter 6 is twofold: first, to show how to generate a price index, and second, to explain how to employ a price index to compare dollar figures from different points in time and to adjust interest rates for inflation. In addition, some of the shortcomings of using the consumer price index as a measure of the cost of living are explained.

B. Helpful Hints

1. *A person's particular consumption basket may not be typical.* Because the gross domestic product (GDP) deflator and the consumer price index (CPI) are based on different baskets of goods and services, each will provide a slightly different measurement of the cost of living. Continuing in this same line of thinking, a person's particular consumption basket may differ from the typical consumption basket used by Statistics Canada when it calculates the CPI. For example, the consumption basket of a young adult may be more heavily weighted toward electronics and clothing. If clothing prices are rising faster than average, young people may have a greater increase in the cost of living than is suggested by the CPI. In like manner, the consumption basket of an old person may be more heavily weighted toward home-care medical services and travel. Above-average increases in these prices may cause the cost of living for the elderly to rise more quickly than suggested by the CPI.

2. *Dollar values can be adjusted backward in time as well as forward.* For example, suppose Karen earned an income of $20 000 in 1990 and $36 000 in 2009.

   The CPI in 1990 (base year 2002) was 78.4 and the CPI in 2009 was 114.4. Karen's 1990 salary can be converted into 2009 dollars as follows:

$$\$20\ 000 \times (114.4/78.4) = \$29\ 183$$

   Her $20 000 salary in 1990 would buy as much as a $29 183 salary in 2009. Because Karen earned $36 000 in 2009, her real income and standard of living rose over those 19 years.

Alternatively, Karen's 2009 salary can be converted into 1990 dollars as follows:

$$\$36\,000 \times (78.4/114.4) = \$24\,671.$$

Karen's $36 000 salary in 2009 would buy as much as a $24 671 salary in 1990. Because she earned $20 000 in 1990, Karen's real income and standard of living were higher in 2009.

3. *When correcting interest rates for inflation, think like a lender.* If Karen loans someone $100 for one year, and she charges 7 percent interest, she will receive $107 at the end of the year. Did Karen receive 7 additional dollars of purchasing power? Suppose inflation was 4 percent. She would need to receive $104 at the end of the year just to break even. That is, Karen would need $104 just to be able to buy the same set of goods and services that she could have purchased for $100 at the time she granted the loan. In this sense, Karen received only three additional dollars of purchasing power for having made the $100 loan, or a 3 percent real return. Thus, the *real interest rate* on the loan is 3 percent, using the formula:

$$7\% - 4\% = 3\%$$

Although not explicitly stated, the interest rate example in the text is also approached from the lender's perspective. That is, when a person deposits money in a bank and receives interest, the deposit is actually a loan from the depositor to the bank.

II. Self-Testing Challenges

A. True/False Questions

_____ 1.   An increase in the price of imported cameras is captured by the CPI but not by the GDP deflator.

_____ 2.   An increase in the price of helicopters purchased by the Canadian military is captured by the CPI.

_____ 3.   Because an increase in gasoline prices causes consumers to ride their bikes more and drive their cars less, the CPI tends to underestimate the cost of living.

_____ 4.   An increase in the price of diamonds will have a greater impact on the CPI than an equal percentage increase in the price of food because diamonds are so much more expensive.

_____ 5.   The rate of core inflation excludes the most volatile components from the CPI basket.

_____ 6.   If the CPI rises at 5 percent per year, then every individual in the country needs exactly a 5 percent increase in their income for their standard of living to remain constant.

_____7.   The GDP deflator is constructed to measure the change in price of domestically produced goods and services.

_____8.   If Statistics Canada fails to recognize that recently produced automobiles can be driven for many more kilometres than older models, then the CPI tends to overestimate the cost of living.

_____9.   If a worker's wage rises from $9.00 to $10.30 while the CPI rises from 112 to 121, the worker should feel an increase in standard of living.

_____10.   The largest category of goods and services in the CPI is transportation.

_____11.   It is impossible for *real* interest rates to be negative.

_____12.   If the nominal interest rate is 12 percent and the rate of inflation is 7 percent, then the real rate of interest is 5 percent.

_____13.   If lenders demand a real rate of return of 4 percent and they expect inflation to be 5 percent, then they should charge 9 percent interest when they extend loans.

_____14.   If borrowers and lenders agree on a nominal interest rate, and inflation turns out to be greater than they had anticipated, lenders will gain at the expense of borrowers.

_____15.   If workers and firms agree on an increase in wages based on their expectations of inflation, and inflation turns out to be less than they expected, workers will gain at the expense of firms.

B. Multiple-Choice Questions

1. Which one of the following is a measure of inflation?
   a. GDP deflator
   b. nominal GDP
   c. real GDP
   d. real rate of interest

2. Which one of the following would have the **MOST** influence on CPI?
   a. a 10 percent increase in the price of food
   b. a 10 percent increase in the price of shelter
   c. a 10 percent increase in the price of transportation
   d. a 10 percent increase in the price of health and personal care

3. In 2005, the CPI was 107.0. In 2006, it was 109.1. Which one of the following was the rate of inflation for 2006?
   a. 1.8 percent
   b. 2.0 percent
   c. 2.2 percent

4. Which one of the following would cause the CPI to rise more than the GDP deflator?
    a. an increase in the price of agricultural machinery
    b. an increase in the price of tanks purchased by the military
    c. an increase in the price of Hondas produced in Japan and sold in Canada
    d. an increase in the price of domestically produced telecommunications equipment sold exclusively to the United States

5. Which one of the following describes the composition of the "basket" on which the CPI is based?
    a. consumer production
    b. total current production
    c. raw materials purchased by firms
    d. products purchased by the typical consumer

6. Suppose there is an increase in the price of apples that causes consumers to purchase fewer kilograms of apples and more kilograms of oranges. Which one of the following will the CPI suffer from?
    a. base-year bias
    b. substitution bias
    c. bias due to unmeasured quality change
    d. bias due to the introduction of new goods

Use the following table for questions 7–12. The table shows the prices and the quantities consumed in Carnivore Country. The base year is 2008. (This is also the year the typical consumption basket was determined.)

Year	Price of beef	Quantity of beef	Price of pork	Quantity of pork
2008	$2.00	100	$1.00	100
2009	$2.50	90	$0.90	120
2010	$2.75	105	$1.00	130

7. Which one of the following is the value of the basket in the base year?
    a. $300
    b. $333
    c. $418.75
    d. $459.25

8. Which one of the following lists the values of the CPI in 2008, 2009, and 2010, respectively?
    a. 100, 111, 139.6
    b. 100, 109.2, 116
    c. 100, 113.3, 125
    d. 83.5, 94.2, 100

9. Which one of the following is the inflation rate for 2009?
   a. 0 percent
   b. 9.2 percent
   c. 11 percent
   d. 13.3 percent

10. Which one of the following is the inflation rate for 2010?
    a. 0 percent
    b. 10.3 percent
    c. 11 percent
    d. 13.3 percent

11. Which one of the following explains why the table shows that the 2009 inflation rate is biased upward?
    a. because of base-year bias
    b. because of substitution bias
    c. because of bias due to unmeasured quality change
    d. because of bias due to the introduction of new goods

12. Suppose the base year is changed in the table from 2008 to 2010 (now use the 2010 consumption basket). Which one of the following is the new value of the CPI in 2009?
    a. 90.6
    b. 100.0
    c. 114.7
    d. 134.3

13. Suppose Peter's income rises from $29 000 to $46 000 while the CPI rises from 122 to 169. Which one of the following has likely occurred to Peter's standard of living?
    a. It has likely fallen.
    b. It has likely risen.
    c. It has likely stayed the same.

14. If the nominal interest rate is 7 percent and the inflation rate is 3 percent, which one of the following is the real interest rate?
    a. −4 percent
    b. 3 percent
    c. 4 percent
    d. 10 percent

15. Which one of the following statements is correct?
    a. The real interest rate is the sum of the nominal interest rate and the inflation rate.
    b. The real interest rate is the nominal interest rate minus the inflation rate.
    c. The nominal interest rate is the inflation rate minus the real interest rate.
    d. The nominal interest rate is the real interest rate minus the inflation rate.

16. If inflation is 8 percent and the real interest rate is 3 percent, then which one of the following should be the nominal interest rate?
    a. 3 percent
    b. 5 percent
    c. 11 percent
    d. 24 percent

17. Which one of the following describes conditions under which it is preferable to be the lender?
    a. The nominal rate of interest is 20 percent and the inflation rate is 25 percent.
    b. The nominal rate of interest is 15 percent and the inflation rate is 14 percent.
    c. The nominal rate of interest is 12 percent and the inflation rate is 9 percent.
    d. The nominal rate of interest is 5 percent and the inflation rate is 1 percent.

18. Which one of the following describes conditions under which it is preferable to be the borrower?
    a. The nominal rate of interest is 20 percent and the inflation rate is 25 percent.
    b. The nominal rate of interest is 15 percent and the inflation rate is 14 percent.
    c. The nominal rate of interest is 12 percent and the inflation rate is 9 percent.
    d. The nominal rate of interest is 5 percent and the inflation rate is 1 percent.

19. Which one of the following will occur if borrowers and lenders agree on a nominal interest rate, and inflation turns out to be less than they had expected?
    a. Borrowers will gain at the expense of lenders.
    b. Lenders will gain at the expense of borrowers.
    c. Neither borrowers nor lenders will gain because the nominal interest rate has been fixed by contract.

20. Which one of the following will occur if workers and firms agree on an increase in wages based on their expectations of inflation, and inflation turns out to be more than they expected?
    a. Firms will gain at the expense of workers.
    b. Workers will gain at the expense of firms.
    c. Neither workers nor firms will gain because the increase in wages is fixed in the labour agreement.

C. Short-Answer Questions

1. What does the consumer price index attempt to measure? _____

2. What are the steps that one must go through in order to construct a consumer price index?_____
_____
_____

3. Which would have a greater impact on the CPI: a 20 percent increase in the price of Rolex watches or a 20 percent increase in the price of new cars? Why? _____

    _____

4. Suppose there is an increase in the price of Honda automobiles imported from Japan. Would this have a larger impact on the CPI or the GDP deflator? Why?

    _____

    _____

    _____

5. If Statistics Canada failed to recognize the increase in memory, power, and speed of newer model computers, in which direction would the CPI be biased? What is this type of bias called? _____

    _____

6. What does the real interest rate measure? _____

    _____

7. Suppose Melvin lends money to his sister at a nominal interest rate of 10 percent because they both expect the inflation rate to be 6 percent. Further, suppose that after the loan has been repaid, Melvin discovers that the actual inflation rate over the life of the loan was only 2 percent. Who gained at the other's expense: Melvin or his sister? Why? _____

    _____

    _____

    _____

8. Paying close attention to Question 7, make a general statement with regard to who gains or loses (the borrower or the lender) on a loan contract when inflation turns out to be either higher or lower than expected.

    _____

    _____

    _____

9. If workers and firms negotiate a wage increase based on their expectation of inflation, who gains or loses (the workers or the firms) if actual inflation turns out to be higher than expected? Why? _____

    _____

    _____

D. Practice Problems

1. The following table shows the prices and the quantities consumed in the country known as College Canada. Suppose the base year is 2008. (This is also the year the typical consumption basket was determined.)

Year	Price of books	Quantity of books	Price of pencils	Quantity of pencils	Price of pens	Quantity of pens
2008	$50	10	$1	100	$5	100
2009	$50	12	$1	200	$10	50
2010	$60	12	$1.50	250	$20	20

a. What is the value of the CPI in 2008?_____

b. What is the value of the CPI in 2009?_____

c. What is the value of the CPI in 2010?_____

d. What is the inflation rate in 2009?_____

e. What is the inflation rate in 2010?_____

f. What type of bias do you observe in the CPI and corresponding inflation rates you generated above? Explain. _____

_____

_____

g. If workers had a COLA clause in their wage contract based on the CPI calculated above, would their standard of living likely increase, decrease, or stay the same over the years 2008–2010? Why?_____

_____

_____

h. If Davis personally consumes only pens (no books or pencils), would his standard of living likely increase, decrease, or stay the same over the years 2008–2010? Why?_____

_____

_____

2. The following table contains the CPI (base year 2002) and the average hourly earnings of Canadian workers for the period 2000–2009.

Year	CPI	Average hourly earnings ($)
2000	95.4	16.49
2001	97.8	16.78
2002	100.0	17.08
2003	102.8	17.20
2004	104.7	17.73
2005	107.0	18.30
2006	109.1	18.76
2007	111.5	19.48
2008	114.1	20.16
2009	114.4	20.44

a.

Inflate the 2000 average hourly earnings to its equivalent value measured in 2009 prices. _____

_____

_____

b.

What happened to real average hourly earnings over this 9-year period?

_____

_____

c.

Deflate the 2009 average hourly earnings to its equivalent value measured in 2000 prices._____

_____

_____

d.

Do these two methods provide consistent answers with respect to real average hourly earnings over this 9-year period?_____

_____

_____

3. Suppose that Yolanda lends her roommate $100 for one year at 9 percent nominal interest.

a. How many dollars of interest will the roommate pay Yolanda at the end of the year? _____

b. Suppose at the time they agreed to the terms of the loan, they both expected the inflation rate to be 5 percent during the year of the loan. What do they both expect the real interest rate to be on the loan?

_____

c. Suppose at the end of the year, Yolanda is surprised to discover that the actual inflation rate over the year was 8 percent. What was the actual real interest rate generated by this loan? _____

d. In the case described above, actual inflation turned out to be higher than expected. Who had the unexpected gain or loss? The roommate (the borrower), or Yolanda (the lender)? Why? _____

_____

_____

e. What would the real interest rate on the loan have been if the actual inflation rate had turned out to be a whopping 11 percent? _____

_____

f. Explain what it means to have a negative real interest rate. _____

_____

_____

_____

E. Advanced Critical Thinking

Joan's father stopped drinking beer in 2005. When she asked him why he stopped, he said, "I stopped because it was just getting too expensive. In 1990, beer was only $24.00 per case. The last case I bought in 2005 was $32.00, and I just couldn't justify spending $8.00 more on a case of beer."

1. In 1990 the CPI was 78.4. In 2005 the CPI was 107.0. What is wrong with his explanation? _____

_____

_____

2. What is the equivalent cost of a 1990 case of beer measured in 2005 prices?

_____

_____

3. What is the equivalent cost of a 2005 case of beer measured in 1990 prices?

_____

_____

_____

4. Do both methods provide the same conclusion?_____

_____

_____

5. The preceding example demonstrates what economists refer to as "money illusion." Why would economists choose the phrase "money illusion" to describe this behaviour? _____

_____

_____

_____

a. Plot the supply and demand for loanable funds. What is the equilibrium real interest rate and the equilibrium level of saving and investment?

_____
_____
_____
_____

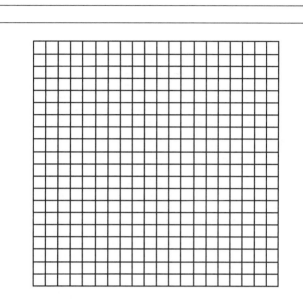

b. What "market forces" will not allow 2 percent to be the real interest rate?

_____
_____
_____
_____

c. Suppose the government suddenly increases its budget deficit by $40 billion. What is the new equilibrium real interest rate and equilibrium level of saving and investment? Explain and show graphically. _____

_____
_____
_____

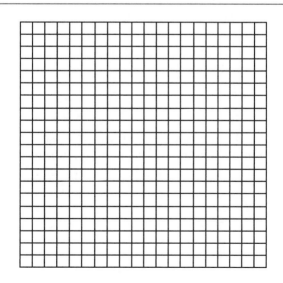

d. Starting at the original equilibrium, suppose the government enacts an investment tax credit that stimulates the demand for loanable funds for capital investment by $40 billion at any real interest rate. What is the new equilibrium real interest rate and equilibrium level of saving and investment? Explain and show graphically._____

_____

_____

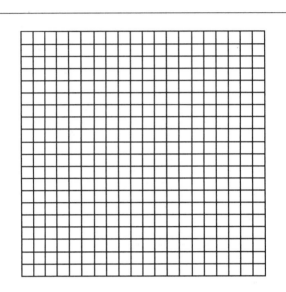

e. With regard to (c) and (d), which policy is **MOST** likely to increase growth? Why? _____

_____

_____

_____

E. Advanced Critical Thinking

During a political debate, a candidate is questioned about her position on economic growth. She says, "We need to get this country growing again. We need to use tax cuts to stimulate saving and investment, and we need to get that budget deficit down so that the government stops absorbing our nation's saving."

1. If government spending remains unchanged, what inconsistency is implied by the candidate's statement? _____

_____

_____

2. If the candidate truly wishes to decrease taxes and decrease the budget deficit, what has she implied about her plans for government spending?_____

_____

_____

3. If policymakers want to increase growth, and if policymakers have to choose between tax incentives to stimulate saving and tax incentives to stimulate investment, what might they want to know about supply and demand in the loanable funds market before making their decision? Explain.

_____
_____
_____
_____
_____
_____

III. Solutions

A. True/False Questions

1. F; to sell a bond is to engage in debt finance.
2. F; stockholders are owners.
3. T
4. T
5. T
6. F; public saving is negative when a government budget deficit exists.
7. T
8. T
9. F; consumption loans do not increase national saving.
10. T
11. F; desired lending exceeds desired borrowing.
12. T
13. T
14. F; it should lower taxes on interest and dividends.
15. F; it decreases the supply of loanable funds.

B. Multiple-Choice Questions

1. a	5. c	9. c	13. c	17. b
2. b	6. b	10. d	14. a	18. b
3. d	7. a	11. b	15. b	
4. a	8. a	12. a	16. b	

C. Short-Answer Questions

1. Because a mutual fund is diversified. When one stock in the fund is performing poorly, it is likely that another stock is performing well.

2. A corporate bond, because the bond is riskier and because "direct" lending through a financial market has fewer overhead costs than "indirect" lending through an intermediary.

3. Debt finance is borrowing, such as when a firm sells a bond. Equity finance is taking on additional partners, such as when a firm sells stock.

4. Saving is what remains after consumption and government purchases. Investment is the purchase of equipment and structures. In casual conversation, saving is what remains of a person's income after consumption, and investment is the purchase of stocks and bonds.

5. Because saving is the GDP left over after consumption expenditures and government purchases, and this is the limit of the income available for purchasing equipment and structures.

6. Private saving = Y – T – C. Public saving = T – G.

7. Public saving would decrease and cause national saving and investment to decrease by the same amount, slowing growth.

8. The supply of loanable funds would shift right, the real interest rate would fall, and the quantity of loanable funds demanded to purchase capital would increase. Growth would increase.

9. The supply of loanable funds would shift right, the real interest rate would fall, and the quantity of loanable funds demanded to purchase capital would increase. Growth would increase.

10. The demand for loanable funds is defined as *private* demand for borrowing to purchase capital equipment and structures. An increase in a deficit absorbs saving and reduces the supply of loanable funds.

D. Practice Problems

1. a. Long-term, because it is more likely that Sven may need to sell the long-term bond before maturity at a depressed price.
    b. Yes, the credit risk has increased and lenders would demand a higher rate of return.
    c. Owners of stock demand a higher rate of return because stocks are riskier.
    d. It is safer to put money in a mutual fund because it is diversified (i.e., not all of one's eggs in one basket).

2. a. ($600 – $100 – $400) + ($100 – $120) = $80 billion
    b. $600 – $100 – $400 = $100 billion
    c. $100 – $120 = –$20 billion
    d. It is harming growth because public saving is negative, therefore less national saving is available for investment.
    e. Because politicians cannot agree on whether to increase taxes or decrease spending.

3.   a.   Equilibrium real interest rate = 4%. Equilibrium S and I = $100 billion.

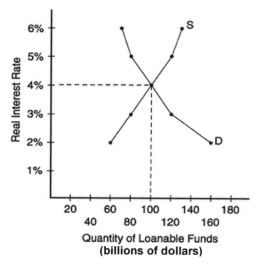

   b.   At 2 percent interest, the quantity demanded of loanable funds exceeds the
        quantity supplied by $90 billion. This excess demand for loans
        (borrowing) will drive interest rates up to 4 percent.

   c.   Equilibrium real interest rate = 5%. Equilibrium S and I = $80 billion.

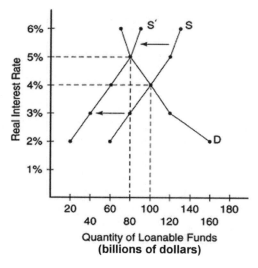

d. Equilibrium real interest rate = 5%. Equilibrium S and I = $120 billion.

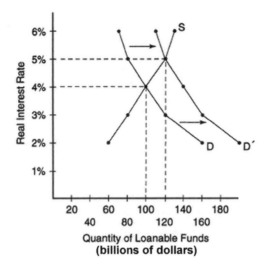

e. An investment tax credit, because it shifts the demand for loanable funds to invest in capital to the right, thus raising the level of investment in capital and stimulating growth.

E. Advanced Critical Thinking

1. Tax cuts to stimulate saving and investment would increase the deficit, which would reduce national saving and investment.

2. The candidate plans to reduce government spending by even more than she cuts taxes.

3. Policymakers would want to know the elasticity of the supply and demand curves. If loanable funds demand is inelastic, changes in loanable funds supply have little effect on saving and investment, therefore tax incentives to increase saving at each interest rate do little for growth. If loanable funds supply is inelastic, changes in loanable funds demand have little effect on saving and investment, therefore tax incentives to increase investment at each interest rate do little for growth.

9 Unemployment and Its Natural Rate

I. Chapter Overview

A. Context and Purpose

Chapter 9 is the third chapter in a three-chapter sequence on the level and growth of output in the long run. In Chapter 7, we learned that capital and labour are among the primary determinants of output and growth. In Chapter 8, we addressed how saving and investment in capital goods affect the production of output. Here in Chapter 9, we see how full utilization of our labour resources improves the level of production and our standard of living.

The purpose of Chapter 9 is to introduce the labour market. It explains how economists measure the performance of the labour market with unemployment statistics. Chapter 9 also examines the four factors that cause unemployment in the long run, and the effects of government policies on the natural rate of unemployment.

B. Helpful Hints

1. *Job search takes time even at the competitive equilibrium wage.* Minimum-wage laws, unions, and efficiency wages all create an excess supply of labour, called structural unemployment, by holding the wage above the competitive equilibrium wage. However, the frictional unemployment that arises from the process of job search occurs at the competitive equilibrium wage because it is inevitable that it takes time for workers and firms to match, regardless of the wage.

2. *The natural rate of unemployment is persistent, not constant.* Minimum-wage laws, unions, efficiency wages, and job search all have impacts on the natural rate of unemployment. Therefore, the natural rate of unemployment will change as government policies, institutions, and behaviours change. But because policies, institutions, and behaviours change slowly, so does the natural rate of unemployment. Note then, that the natural rate of unemployment is estimated to have been as low as 4 percent in the late 1960s, and as high as 8 percent in the late 1980s.

II. Self-Testing Challenges

A. True/False Questions

____ 1.   The natural rate of unemployment is the amount of unemployment that will not go away on its own, even in the long run.

____ 2.   If the unemployment rate falls, it is certain that more workers have jobs.

_____3.   In post-World War II Canada, the labour-force participation rate has been rising for women and has been falling for men.

_____4.   The unemployment rate is about the same for Atlantic Canada and Western Canada.

_____5.   A minimum wage is likely to have a greater impact on the market for skilled workers than on the market for unskilled workers.

_____6.   The presence of a union tends to raise the wage for insiders and lower the wage for outsiders.

_____7.   A union is a labour cartel.

_____8.   Unions may increase efficiency in some circumstances because they decrease the cost of bargaining between labour and management.

_____9.   An efficiency wage is like a minimum wage in that firms are required by legislation to pay it.

_____10.   Paying efficiency wages tends to increase worker turnover because workers can get continually higher wages if they "job hop."

_____11.   If a firm pays above the competitive equilibrium wage, its worker pool may increase because better quality candidates tend to apply for the firm's job openings.

_____12.   If wages were always at the competitive equilibrium, there would be absolutely no unemployment.

_____13.   If there are "discouraged searchers," the measured unemployment rate overstates true unemployment.

_____14.   The existence of Employment Insurance tends to decrease the unemployment rate because recipients of insurance benefits are not counted in the labour force.

_____15.   Whenever the wage rises above the competitive equilibrium, regardless of the source, the result is structural unemployment.

B. Multiple-Choice Questions

1.   Which one of the following refers to the amount of unemployment that the economy normally experiences?
   a.   union unemployment
   b.   cyclical unemployment
   c.   efficiency wage unemployment
   d.   natural rate of unemployment

2. According to Statistics Canada, which one of the following refers to a husband who chooses to stay home and take care of the household?
    a. employed
    b. unemployed
    c. not in the labour force
    d. a discouraged searcher

Use the following table for questions 3 through 5.

	Quantity (millions)
Total population	29.7
Adult population	21.2
Unemployed	1.2
Employed	12.1

3. Which one of the following is the size of the labour force?
    a. 12.1 million
    b. 13.3 million
    c. 20.0 million
    d. 21.2 million

4. Which one of the following is the unemployment rate?
    a. 5.7 percent
    b. 6.0 percent
    c. 9.0 percent
    d. 9.9 percent

5. Which one of the following is the labour-force participation rate?
    a. 40.7 percent
    b. 44.8 percent
    c. 57.1 percent
    d. 62.7 percent

6. Which one of the following refers to a person with a CA designation who has been unable to find work for so long that she has stopped looking for work?
    a. She is considered to be employed.
    b. She is considered to be unemployed.
    c. She is not considered to be in the labour force.
    d. She is not considered to be in the adult population.

7. Which one of the following statements is true?
    a. The labour-force participation rate of men is rising.
    b. Women tend to have a lower labour-force participation rate than men.
    c. Younger workers tend to have lower unemployment rates than older workers.

8. Which one of the following tends to be an effect of the minimum-wage law?
   a. It creates more unemployment in high-skill job markets than in low-skill job markets.
   b. It creates more unemployment in low-skill job markets than in high-skill job markets.
   c. It has no impact on unemployment as long as it is set above the competitive equilibrium wage.
   d. It helps all teenagers because they receive a higher wage than they would otherwise.

9. Which of the following sources of unemployment is **NOT** based on the wage being held above the competitive equilibrium wage?
   a. unemployment due to unions
   b. unemployment due to job search
   c. unemployment due to efficiency wages
   d. unemployment due to minimum-wage laws

10. Which one of the following will result if, for any reason, the wage is held above the competitive equilibrium wage?
    a. Unions will likely strike and the wage will fall to equilibrium.
    b. The quality of workers will fall due to the change in the number of workers in the applicant pool.
    c. The quantity of labour demanded will exceed the quantity of labour supplied and there will be a labour shortage.
    d. The quantity of labour supplied will exceed the quantity of labour demanded and there will be structural unemployment.

11. Which one of the following defines efficiency wage?
    a. the competitive equilibrium wage
    b. the above-equilibrium wage paid by firms
    c. the minimum wage the firm is willing to pay
    d. the minimum wage the worker is willing to accept

12. Which one of the following government policies would increase the unemployment rate?
    a. raising the minimum wage
    b. establishing employment agencies
    c. establishing worker training programs
    d. reducing Employment Insurance benefits

13. Which one of the following types of unemployment tends to be raised by sectoral shifts?
    a. frictional unemployment
    b. structural unemployment
    c. cyclical unemployment

14. Which one of the following is **NOT** a reason why firms may want to pay high wages?
    a. improved worker health
    b. increased worker turnover
    c. increased worker effort
    d. improved worker quality

15. Which one of the following countries has the **LOWEST** rate of union membership?
    a. Canada
    b. Sweden
    c. Denmark
    d. United States

16. Which one of the following describes how unions might increase efficiency?
    a. By lowering the wage of local outsiders.
    b. By offsetting the market power of a large firm in a company town.
    c. By raising the wage for insiders above the competitive equilibrium.
    d. By threatening a strike but not actually following through, therefore no hours of work are lost.

17. Which one of the following statements about efficiency wage theory is true?
    a. Paying the lowest possible wage is always the most efficient (profitable).
    b. Paying above the competitive equilibrium wage causes workers to shirk their responsibilities.
    c. Firms do not have a choice about whether they pay efficiency wages or not because these wages are determined by law.
    d. Paying above the competitive equilibrium wage may improve worker health, lower worker turnover, improve worker quality, and increase worker effort.

18. Which one of the following describes how unions tend to increase the disparity in pay between insiders and outsiders?
    a. By increasing the demand for workers in the unionized sector
    b. By decreasing the demand for workers in the unionized sector
    c. By increasing the wage in the unionized sector, which may create an increase in the supply of workers in the nonunionized sector
    d. By increasing the wage in the unionized sector, which may create a decrease in the supply of workers in the nonunionized sector

19. Which one of the following types of unemployment will exist even if the wage is at the competitive equilibrium?
    a. unemployment due to unions
    b. unemployment due to job search
    c. unemployment due to efficiency wages
    d. unemployment due to minimum-wage laws

20. Which one of the following would occur if Employment Insurance benefits were so generous that laid-off workers would be paid 95 percent of their regular salary?
    a. Frictional unemployment would fall.
    b. There would be no impact on measured unemployment.
    c. Measured unemployment would probably understate true unemployment.
    d. Measured unemployment would probably overstate true unemployment.

C. Short-Answer Questions

1. Give two reasons why the unemployment rate is an imperfect measure of joblessness. _____

    _____
    _____
    _____

2. Where would a labour union be more likely to increase efficiency rather than reduce it: in a small, remote town with one large employer, or in a major city with many employers? Why? _____

    _____
    _____

3. Describe two ways that a union increases the disparity in the wages of members and nonmembers._____

    _____
    _____

4. Does the minimum wage cause much unemployment in the market for accountants? Why or why not?

    _____
    _____
    _____

5. Which type of unemployment will occur even if the wage is at the competitive equilibrium? Why? _____

    _____
    _____
    _____

6. How does Employment Insurance increase frictional unemployment? _____

    _____
    _____
    _____

7. How might the government help reduce frictional unemployment?_____

    _____
    _____
    _____

8. Which of the following individuals is **MOST** likely to be unemployed for the long term: a fisherman who loses his job when the fish stocks decline, or a waitress who is laid off when a new cafe opens in town? Why?

_____

_____

_____

D. Practice Problems

1. Use the following information about Country A to answer all parts of this question.

	2009 (millions)	2010 (millions)
Population	223.6	226.5
Adult population	168.2	169.5
Unemployed	7.4	8.1
Employed	105.2	104.2

a. How many people were in the labour force in 2009? How many people were in the labour force in 2010? _____

_____

_____

b. What was the labour-force participation rate in 2009? What was the labour-force participation rate in 2010? _____

_____

_____

c. What was the unemployment rate in 2009? What was the unemployment rate in 2010? _____

_____

_____

d. From 2009 to 2010, the adult population went up while the labour force went down. Provide a number of explanations why this might have occurred._____

_____

_____

_____

_____

e. If the natural rate of unemployment in Country A is 6.6 percent, how much is cyclical unemployment in 2009 and 2010? Is Country A likely to be experiencing a recession in either of these years?

_____

_____

_____

_____

_____

exchange rate is two-thirds German Big Mac per one Canadian Big Mac.

_____12.   In order to increase domestic investment, a country must either increase its saving or decrease its net capital outflow.

_____13.   Arbitrage is the process of taking advantage of differences in prices of the same good by buying it from a market where the good is cheap and selling it in another market where the good is expensive.

_____14.   Canadian real interest rates have been higher than U.S. real interest rates partly because of higher tax rates in Canada.

_____15.   If a company based in Canada prefers a strong Canadian dollar (a dollar with a high exchange value), it must export more than it imports.

B. Multiple-Choice Questions

1.   Which one of the following terms refers to an economy that interacts with other economies?
   a.   a balanced trade economy
   b.   an export economy
   c.   an import economy
   d.   an open economy

2.   Which one of the following is **NOT** a reason why the Canadian economy continues to engage in greater amounts of international trade?
   a.   There are larger cargo ships and airplanes.
   b.   High-technology goods are more valuable per kilogram, and thus more likely to be traded.
   c.   NAFTA imposes requirements for increased trade between countries in North America.
   d.   There have been improvements in technology that have improved telecommunications between countries.

3.   Which one of the following statements is true about a country with a trade deficit?
   a.   Net exports are negative.
   b.   Exports exceed imports.
   c.   Net capital outflow must be positive.
   d.   The current account balance must be positive.

4.   Which one of the following developments would directly increase Canadian net capital outflow?
   a.   Honda builds a new plant in Ontario.
   b.   Air Canada buys a new plane from the United States.
   c.   Toyota buys stock in the Bank of Montreal.
   d.   Research In Motion builds a new distribution facility in Sweden.

5. Which one of the following is correct if Japan exports more than it imports?
   a. Japan is running a trade deficit.
   b. Japan's net exports are negative.
   c. Japan's net capital outflow must be positive.
   d. Japan's current account balance must be negative

6. If Canada saves $100 billion and Canadian net capital outflow is −$20 billion, what is the value of Canadian domestic investment?
   a. −$20 billion
   b. $20 billion
   c. $80 billion
   d. $120 billion

7. Which one of the following is true if the exchange rate changes from 3 Euros per dollar to 4 Euros per dollar?
   a. The dollar has depreciated.
   b. The dollar has appreciated.
   c. The dollar could have appreciated or depreciated depending on what happened to relative prices in Europe and Canada.

8. Suppose the real exchange rate between Russia and Canada is defined in terms of bottles of Russian vodka per bottle of Canadian vodka. Which one of the following will increase the real exchange rate (that is, increase the number of bottles of Russian vodka per bottle of Canadian vodka)?
   a. An increase in the Ruble price of Russian vodka.
   b. An increase in the dollar price of Canadian vodka.
   c. A decrease in the number of Rubles for which the dollar can be exchanged.

9. Which one of the following is the **MOST** accurate measure of the international value of the dollar?
   a. the yen-per-dollar exchange rate
   b. the euro-per-dollar exchange rate
   c. the U.S.-dollar-per-Canadian-dollar exchange rate
   d. an exchange rate index that accounts for many exchange rates

10. If the nominal exchange rate between British pounds and Canadian dollars is 0.5 pound per dollar, which one of the following is the amount of Canadian dollars you can get for a British pound?
    a. 0.5 of a dollar
    b. 1 dollar
    c. 1.5 dollars
    d. 2 dollars

11. Suppose the nominal exchange rate between the Mexican peso and the Canadian dollar is 10 pesos per dollar. Further, suppose that a kilogram of hamburger costs $2 in Canada and 25 pesos in Mexico. Which one of the following is the real exchange rate between Mexico and Canada?
    a. 0.5 kg of Mexican hamburger per 1 kg of Canadian hamburger
    b. 0.8 kg of Mexican hamburger per 1 kg of Canadian hamburger

    c. 1.25 kg of Mexican hamburger per 1 kg of Canadian hamburger
    d. 2.5 kg of Mexican hamburger per 1 kg of Canadian hamburger

12.   Which one of the following people would be pleased by a depreciation of the Canadian dollar?
    a. a Canadian tourist traveling in Europe
    b. a Canadian importer of Russian vodka
    c. a French exporter of wine to Canada
    d. an Italian importer of Canadian steel

13.   Suppose a cup of coffee costs 1.5 Euros in Germany and $0.50 in Canada. If purchasing-power parity holds, which one of the following is the nominal exchange rate between Euros and dollars?
    a. one-third of a euro per dollar
    b. 0.75 Euros per dollar
    c. 1.5 Euros per dollar
    d. 3 Euros per dollar

14.   Which one of the following products would likely be the **LEAST** accurate if used to calculate purchasing-power parity?
    a. gold
    b. automobiles
    c. diamonds
    d. dental services

15.   Suppose the money supply in Mexico grows more quickly than the money supply in Canada. Which one of the following is the expected result?
    a. The peso should depreciate relative to the dollar.
    b. The peso should appreciate relative to the dollar.
    c. The peso should maintain a constant exchange rate with the dollar because of purchasing-power parity.

16.   Suppose a resident of Canada buys a Jaguar automobile from Great Britain and the British exporter uses the receipts to buy stock in Toronto Dominion Bank. Which one of the following statements is true from the perspective of Canada?
    a. Net exports fall and net capital outflow falls.
    b. Net exports rise and net capital outflow rises.
    c. Net exports fall and net capital outflow rises.
    d. Net exports rise and net capital outflow falls.

17.   Which one of the following statements is **NOT** true about the relationship between national saving, investment, and net capital outflow?
    a. Saving is the sum of investment and net capital outflow.
    b. For a given amount of saving, an increase in net capital outflow must decrease domestic investment.
    c. For a given amount of saving, a decrease in net capital outflow must decrease domestic investment.
    d. An increase in saving associated with an equal increase in net capital outflow leaves domestic investment unchanged.

18. Suppose the inflation rate over the last 20 years has been 9 percent in Great Britain, 7 percent in Japan, and 5 percent in Canada. If purchasing-power parity holds, which one of the following statements describes the most likely result?

   a. Over this period, the value of the dollar should have fallen compared to the value of the pound and the yen.

   b. Over this period, the yen should have risen in value compared to the pound and fallen compared to the dollar.

   c. Over this period, the yen should have fallen in value compared to the pound and risen compared to the dollar.

   d. Over this period, the value of the pound should have risen compared to the value of the yen and the dollar.

19. If the interest rate in Canada equals the interest rate prevailing in world financial markets, which one of the following is this a result of?
   a. net exports
   b. net capital outflow
   c. interest-rate parity
   d. purchasing-power parity

20. If the world interest rate is 6 percent and foreigners believe that there is a higher default risk in Canada, then what is the expected interest rate in Canada?
   a. more than 6 percent.
   b. 6 percent.
   c. less than 6 percent.

C. Short-Answer Questions

1. Identify four reasons why the Canadian economy has engaged in an increasing amount of trade over the last 40 years. _____
   _____
   _____
   _____

2. Define net capital outflow. When foreigners invest in Canada, what happens to the value of Canadian NCO? _____
   _____
   _____

3. What are the two mutually exclusive locations where national saving can be invested? _____
   _____

4. If national saving is held constant, what happens to domestic investment if NCO decreases? Why? _____
   _____

5. Define the current account balance. When foreigners receive interest and dividends on their holdings of Canadian bonds and stocks, what happens to the current account balance? _____

    _____

    _____

6. In terms of the real exchange rate, what three variables could change to make Canada more competitive internationally? _____

    _____

    _____

7. Suppose a Chrysler minivan sells for CDN$30 000 in Canada, and for US$24 000 in the United States. If purchasing-power parity holds, what is the US$/CDN$ exchange rate? How many Canadian dollars does it take to buy US$1.00? _____

    _____

    _____

8. Suppose trade increases between countries. Would this increase or decrease the predictive accuracy of the purchasing-power parity theory of exchange rate determination? _____

    _____

    _____

9. If the money supply grows at an average annual rate of 5 percent in Canada and at an average annual rate of 35 percent in Mexico, what should happen over time to the Mexican-peso-per-dollar exchange rate if purchasing-power parity holds? Why?

    _____

    _____

10. Why might the interest rate in Canada be higher than the interest rate prevailing in world financial markets? _____

    _____

    _____

D. Practice Problems

1. How would each of the following transactions affect Canadian NCO? Does the transaction affect direct investment or portfolio investment?

    a. A Canadian mutual fund buys stock in American Airlines. _____

        _____

    b. Bombardier buys steel from a Japanese manufacturer to use in the production of airplanes._____

        _____

        _____

    c.   Honda expands its plant in Ontario. _____

_____

    d.   A Japanese mutual fund buys shares of stock in Royal Bank. _____

_____

    e.   Research In Motion builds an office in Germany.

_____

_____

2.   Suppose a resident of Great Britain buys a computer from a Canadian manufacturer using British pounds.

    a.   If the Canadian manufacturer holds on to the British pounds, does NX = NCO in this case? Explain. _____

_____

_____

    b.   Suppose the Canadian manufacturer uses the pounds to help build a factory in Great Britain. Does NX = NCO in this case? Explain. What kind of foreign investment is this?

        _____

_____

_____

    c.   Suppose the Canadian manufacturer uses the pounds to buy stock in a British corporation. Does NX = NCO in this case? Explain. What kind of foreign investment is this? _____

_____

_____

    d.   Suppose the Canadian manufacturer uses the pounds to buy computer chips manufactured in Great Britain. Does NX = NCO in this case? Explain.

_____

_____

3.   Suppose the nominal exchange rate is 100 yen per dollar. Further, suppose the price of a baseball glove in Canada is $50 and the price of a baseball glove in Japan is 7500 yen.

    a.   What is the real exchange rate between Japan and Canada in terms of baseball gloves? _____

_____

_____

_____

b.   Is there a profit opportunity that could be exploited with arbitrage? Where would the buying take place and where would the selling take place?

_____

_____

_____

c.   If the nominal exchange rate stayed the same, what should happen to the price of baseball gloves in Canada and Japan? Explain. _____

_____

d.   Suppose prices move. What has happened to the real exchange rate?

_____

_____

4.   Suppose the price of Canadian-bottled spring water is $40 per case in Canada and 600 pesos in Mexico.

a.   What is the nominal peso-per-dollar exchange rate if purchasing-power parity holds?

_____

_____

b.   Suppose Mexico's central bank is politically pressured to double its money supply, which in turn doubles the level of its prices. If purchasing-power parity holds, what is the new peso-per-dollar exchange rate? Did the peso appreciate or depreciate?

_____

_____

c.   Suppose the Bank of Canada now doubles the Canadian money supply, which in turn doubles the level of Canadian prices. If purchasing-power parity holds, what is the value of the peso per dollar exchange rate? Did the dollar appreciate or depreciate? _____

_____

_____

d.   Compare your answers to part (a) and part (c). What has happened to the exchange rate? Why? _____

_____

_____

E. Advanced Critical Thinking

Daniel is watching a national news broadcast with his parents. The news anchor explains that the exchange rate for the dollar just hit its highest value in thirty years. The on-the-spot report shifts to a spokesperson for Research In Motion (RIM), a telecommunications equipment manufacturer. The spokesperson reports that foreign sales of RIM'S telecommunications equipment have fallen sharply. Daniels' parents are shocked by the report's negative view of the high value of the dollar. They just booked their European vacation because of the dollar's high value.

1. Why do RIM and Daniel's parents have different opinions about the value of the dollar? _____

    _____
    _____
    _____

2. RIM imports many parts for its manufacturing processes and it sells many finished products abroad. Because it is upset about a high dollar, what must be true about the amounts of RIM's imports and exports?_

    _____

3. If someone argues that a strong dollar is "good for Canada" because Canadians are able to exchange some of their GDP for a greater amount of foreign GDP, is it true that a strong dollar is good for every Canadian? Why or why not? _____

    _____
    _____

III.   Solutions

A. True/False Questions

1. F; net exports are exports minus imports.
2. T
3. T
4. T
5. T
6. F; if exports exceed imports, the country has a trade surplus.
7. T
8. F; the exchange rate should be 90 yen per dollar.
9. T
10. F; the value of the peso should fall relative to the yen.
11. T
12. T
13. T
14. T
15. F; companies preferring a strong dollar import more than they export.

____13.   A sharp rise in the price of oil can cause stagflation.

____14.   In the long run, an increase in government spending tends to increase
output and prices.

____15.   If policymakers choose to try to move the economy out of a recession, they
should use their policy tools to decrease aggregate demand.

B. Multiple-Choice Questions

1. Which one of the following statements about economic fluctuations is true?
    a. A depression is a mild recession.
    b. A recession is when output rises above the natural rate of output.
    c. Economic fluctuations have been termed the "business cycle" because the
        movements in output are regular and predictable.
    d. A variety of spending, income, and output measures can be used to measure
        economic fluctuations because most macroeconomic quantities tend to
        fluctuate together.

2. Which one of the following would shift the aggregate-demand curve to the right?
    a. a rise in interest rates
    b. a cut in personal income taxes
    c. an exchange rate appreciation
    d. a decrease in government spending on highways

3. Which one of the following would shift the aggregate-demand curve to the left?
    a. a fall in expected future profits by firms
    b. a fall in interest rates
    c. a boom in the stock market
    d. an exchange rate depreciation

4. Which one of the following is **NOT** a reason why the aggregate-demand curve
    slopes downward?
    a. the wealth effect
    b. the interest-rate effect
    c. the real exchange-rate effect
    d. the classical dichotomy/monetary neutrality effects

5. In the model of aggregate supply and aggregate demand, which one of the
    following is the initial impact of an increase in consumer optimism?
    a. a shift of aggregate demand to the left
    b. a shift of aggregate demand to the right
    c. a shift of short-run aggregate supply to the left
    d. a shift of short-run aggregate supply to the right

6. Which one of the following statements describes what occurs in a long-run aggregate-supply curve?
    a. The long-run aggregate-supply curve shifts left when the natural rate of unemployment falls.
    b. The long-run aggregate-supply curve shifts right when the government raises the minimum wage.
    c. The long-run aggregate-supply curve is vertical because an equal change in all prices and wages leaves output unaffected.
    d. The long-run aggregate-supply curve is positively sloped because price expectations and wages tend to be fixed in the long run.

7. Which one of the following is a reason that the aggregate-demand curve slopes downward (negatively), according to the wealth effect?
    a. Lower prices increase the real value of money holdings and consumer spending increases.
    b. Lower prices decrease the real value of money holdings and consumer spending decreases.
    c. Lower prices reduce money holdings and increase lending, interest rates fall, and investment spending increases.
    d. Lower prices increase money holdings and decrease lending, interest rates rise, and investment spending falls.

8. Which one of the following is the natural rate of output?
    a. The amount of real GDP produced when there is no unemployment.
    b. The amount of real GDP produced when the economy is at the natural rate of investment.
    c. The amount of real GDP produced when the economy is at the natural rate of aggregate demand.
    d. The amount of real GDP produced when the economy is at the natural rate of unemployment.

9. Which one of the following refers to a scenario in which the price level falls, but because of fixed nominal wage contracts, the real wage rises and firms cut back on production?
    a. the misperceptions theory of the short-run aggregate-supply curve
    b. the sticky-wage theory of the short-run aggregate-supply curve
    c. the sticky-price theory of the short-run aggregate-supply curve
    d. the classical dichotomy theory of the short-run aggregate-supply curve

10. Suppose the price level falls but suppliers notice only that the price of their particular product has fallen. Thinking there has been a fall in the relative price of their product, they cut back on production. Which one of the following refers to this scenario?
    a. the misperceptions theory of the short-run aggregate-supply curve
    b. the sticky-wage theory of the short-run aggregate-supply curve.
    c. the sticky-price theory of the short-run aggregate-supply curve.
    d. the classical dichotomy theory of the short-run aggregate-supply curve.

11. Suppose the economy is initially in long-run equilibrium. Then suppose there is a reduction in investment spending by firms. According to the model of aggregate demand and aggregate supply, which one of the following is what happens to prices and output in the *short run*?
    a. prices rise, output rises
    b. prices rise, output falls
    c. prices fall, output falls
    d. prices fall, output rises

12. Suppose the economy is initially in long-run equilibrium. Then suppose there is a reduction in investment spending by firms. If the policymakers allow the economy to adjust to long-run equilibrium on its own, according to the model of aggregate demand and aggregate supply, which one of the following is what happens to prices and output in the *long run*?
    a. prices rise, output is unchanged from its initial value
    b. prices fall, output is unchanged from its initial value
    c. output rises, prices are unchanged from the initial value
    d. output falls, prices are unchanged from the initial value
    e. output and the price level are unchanged from their initial values

13. Suppose the economy is initially in long-run equilibrium. Then suppose there is a drought that destroys much of the wheat crop. According to the model of aggregate demand and aggregate supply, which one of the following is what happens to prices and output in the *short run*?
    a. prices rise, output rises
    b. prices rise, output falls
    c. prices fall, output falls
    d. prices fall, output rises

14. Suppose the economy is initially in long-run equilibrium. Then suppose there is a drought that destroys much of the wheat crop. If the policymakers allow the economy to adjust to long-run equilibrium on its own, according to the model of aggregate demand and aggregate supply, what happens to prices and output in the *long run*?
    a. prices rise, output is unchanged from its initial value
    b. prices fall, output is unchanged from its initial value
    c. output rises, prices are unchanged from the initial value
    d. output and the price level are unchanged from their initial values

15. Which one of the following describes when stagflation occurs?
    a. when there are falling prices and falling output
    b. when there are falling prices and rising output
    c. when there are rising prices and rising output
    d. when there are rising prices and falling output

16. Which one of the following events leads to an initial impact that takes the form of a shift in the short-run aggregate-supply curve to the right?
    a. a drop in oil prices
    b. a decrease in the money supply
    c. an increase in price expectations
    d. an increase in government spending on military equipment

17. Suppose the economy is operating in a recession. If policymakers wished to move output to its long-run natural rate, which one of the following should they attempt to do?
    a. shift aggregate demand to the right
    b. shift aggregate demand to the left
    c. shift short-run aggregate supply to the right
    d. shift short-run aggregate supply to the left

18. Suppose the economy is operating in a recession. If policymakers allow the economy to adjust to the long-run natural rate on its own, which one of the following describes the likely outcome?
    a. People will raise their price expectations and aggregate demand will shift left.
    b. People will reduce their price expectations and aggregate demand will shift right.
    c. People will raise their price expectations and the short-run aggregate supply will shift left.
    d. People will reduce their price expectations and the short-run aggregate supply will shift right.

19. According to the model of aggregate supply and aggregate demand, in the long run, which one of the following describes the effects of an increase in the money supply?
    a. It should cause prices to rise and output to rise.
    b. It should cause prices to fall and output to fall.
    c. It should cause prices to rise and output to remain unchanged.
    d. It should cause prices to fall and output to remain unchanged.

20. Which one of the following actions by policymakers is said to "accommodate" an adverse supply shock?
    a. respond to the adverse supply shock by decreasing short-run aggregate supply
    b. fail to respond to the adverse supply shock and allow the economy to adjust on its own
    c. respond to the adverse supply shock by increasing aggregate demand, which further raises prices
    d. respond to the adverse supply shock by decreasing aggregate demand, which lowers prices

C. Short-Answer Questions

1.   Name the three key facts about economic fluctuations._____

_____

_____

2.   Which component of aggregate demand varies the **MOST** over the business cycle?

_____

3.   What happens to the natural rate of output when the natural rate of unemployment falls? _____

_____

4.   What are the three reasons the aggregate-demand curve slopes downward? Explain them. _____

_____

_____

_____

5.   Suppose the economy is in long-run equilibrium. If the sticky-wage theory of the short-run aggregate-supply curve is employed, what initially happens to the real wage if there is a decrease in aggregate demand?

_____

_____

_____

6.   Referring to question 5, if the economy is to adjust on its own back to the long-run equilibrium level of output, what must happen to the real wage?_____

_____

_____

7.   If the economy is in a recession, why might policymakers choose to adjust aggregate demand to eliminate the recession rather than let the economy adjust, or self-correct, on its own? _____

_____

_____

8.   Does a shift in aggregate demand alter output in the long run? Why or why not?_____

_____

_____

9.   Why is money unlikely to be neutral in the short run? _____

_____

10.   How did the model of short-run economic fluctuations develop? _____

_____

_____

D. Practice Problems

1.   Four cases are listed below. Trace the impact of each shock in the aggregate-supply aggregate-demand model by answering the following three questions for each case:

(i) What happens to prices and output in the short run?

(ii) What happens to prices and output in the long run if the economy is allowed to adjust to long-run equilibrium on its own?

(iii) If policymakers had intervened to move output back to the natural rate of output instead of allowing the economy to self-correct, in which direction should they have moved aggregate demand?

a.   aggregate demand shifts left _____

_____

_____

b.   aggregate demand shifts right _____

_____

_____

c.   short-run aggregate supply shifts left _____

_____

_____

d.   short-run aggregate supply shifts right _____

_____

_____

2.   The following events have their *initial impact* on which one of the following: aggregate demand, long-run aggregate supply, or short-run aggregate supply? Does the curve shift to the right or left?

a.   The government repairs aging roads and bridges._____

_____

b.   OPEC raises oil prices.

_____

_____

c.   The government raises Employment Insurance benefits. _____

_____

d.   Canadians feel more secure in their jobs and become more optimistic.

_____

e. A technological advance takes place in the application of computers to the production of steel. _____

_____

f. The government increases the minimum wage.

_____

_____

g. Wage demands of new university graduates fall.

_____

_____

h. The Bank of Canada decreases the money supply.

_____

_____

i. A drought destroys much of the corn crop.

_____

_____

3. Suppose the economy is in long-run equilibrium. Then, suppose the Bank of Canada suddenly increases the money supply.

a. Describe the initial impact of this event in the model of aggregate demand and aggregate supply by explaining which curve shifts which way.

_____

_____

_____

b. What happens to the price level and real output in the short run? _____

_____

_____

c. If the economy is allowed to adjust to the increase in the money supply, what happens to the price level and real output in the long run? (compared to their original levels) _____

_____

d. Does an increase in the money supply move output above the natural rate indefinitely? Why or why not? _____

_____

_____

4.   Suppose the economy is in long-run equilibrium. Then, suppose workers and firms suddenly expect higher prices in the future and agree to an increase in wages.

   a.   Describe the initial impact of this event in the model of aggregate demand and aggregate supply by explaining which curve shifts which way.

_____

_____

_____

   b.   What happens to the price level and real output in the short run?_____

_____

   c.   What name do we have for this combination of movements in output and prices? _____

   d.   If policymakers wanted to move output back to the natural rate of output, what should they do? _____

_____

   e.   If policymakers were able to move output back to the natural rate of output, what would the policy do to prices? _____

_____

   f.   If policymakers did nothing at all, what would happen to the wage rate as the economy self-corrects or adjusts back to the natural rate of output on its own?_____

_____

_____

   g.   Is it likely that an increase in price expectations and wages alone can cause a permanent increase in the price level? Why or why not? _____

_____

_____

5.   Suppose aggregate demand has decreased and the economy is in a recession. Describe the adjustment process necessary for the economy to adjust on its own to the natural rate of output for each of the three theoretical short-run aggregate-supply curves.

   a.   The misperceptions theory: _____

_____

_____

_____

_____

b. The sticky-wage theory: _____

_____

_____

_____

_____

c. The sticky-price theory: _____

_____

_____

_____

_____

d. Would the type of adjustments described above take place more slowly from a recession or from a period when output was above the long-run natural rate? Why? _____

_____

_____

E. Advanced Critical Thinking

Jacquie is watching the evening news on television. The news anchor reports that union wage demands are much higher this year because the workers anticipate an increase in the rate of inflation. Her roommate Estelle says, "Inflation is a self-fulfilling prophecy. If workers think there will be higher prices, they demand higher wages. This increases the cost of production and firms raise their prices. Expecting higher prices simply causes higher prices."

1. Is this true in the short run? Explain._____

_____

_____

_____

2. If policymakers do nothing and allow the economy to adjust to the natural rate of output on its own, does expecting higher prices cause higher prices in the long run? Explain._____

_____

_____

3. If policymakers accommodate the adverse supply shock, does the expectation of higher prices cause higher prices in the long run? Explain._____

_____

_____

_____

III. Solutions

A. True/False Questions

1.   T
2.   T
3.   F; as output falls, unemployment rises.
4.   T
5.   F; fluctuations in output are irregular and unpredictable.
6.   T
7.   F; aggregate demand shifts to the right.
8.   F; it explains why the short-run aggregate-supply curve is upward sloping.
9.   T
10.   F; in a recession, the economy adjusts to long-run equilibrium as wages and price expectations fall.
11.   T
12.   T
13.   T
14.   F; in the long run, it tends to increase prices, but it has no impact on output.
15.   F; policymakers should increase aggregate demand.

B. Multiple-Choice Questions

1. d	5. b	9. b	13. b	17. a
2. c	6. c	10. a	14. d	18. d
3. b	7. a	11. c	15. d	19. c
4. d	8. d	12. b	16. a	20. c

C. Short-Answer Questions

1.   Economic fluctuations are irregular and unpredictable, most macroeconomic quantities fluctuate together, and when output falls, unemployment rises.

2.   Investment spending.

3.   A fall in the natural rate of unemployment would increase the natural rate of output, and shift the long-run aggregate-supply curve to the right.

4.   Wealth effect: lower prices increase the real value of money holdings and consumer spending increases. Interest rate effect: lower prices reduce the quantity of money held, some money is loaned, interest rates fall, and investment spending increases. Real exchange-rate effect: lower prices decrease the real exchange rate, and net exports increase.

5.   Because the nominal wage is fixed for a period, the fall in the price level raises the real wage.

6.   The nominal wage must fall so that the real wage can return to its initial level.

7.   Because they think they can get the economy back to the long-run natural rate of output more quickly or, in the case of a negative supply shock, because they are more concerned with output and employment than inflation.

8.   No. In the long run, output is determined by factor supplies and technology (long-run aggregate supply). Changes in aggregate demand affect output in only the short run because it temporarily alters relative prices.

9.   Because a shift in aggregate demand arising from a change in the money supply may change the price level unexpectedly. Some prices and wages adjust to the change in the price level more quickly than others, which causes changes in relative prices in the short run.

10. The model is a by-product of the Great Depression of the 1930s. In 1936, economist John Maynard Keynes developed the theory that recessions can occur because of inadequate aggregate demand.

D. Practice Problems

1.   a.   Prices fall, output falls. Prices fall, output returns to the natural rate. Shift aggregate demand to the right.

     b.   Prices rise, output rises. Prices rise, output returns to the natural rate. Shift aggregate demand to the left.

     c.   Prices rise, output falls. Price level returns to original value, output returns to the natural rate. Shift aggregate demand to the right.

     d.   Prices fall, output rises. Price level returns to original value, output returns to the natural rate. Shift aggregate demand to the left.

2.   a.   Aggregate demand. Right.

     b.   Short-run aggregate supply. Left.

     c.   Short-run and long-run aggregate supply. Left.

     d.   Aggregate demand. right.

     e.   Short-run and long-run aggregate supply. Right.

     f.   Short-run and long-run aggregate supply. Left.

     g.   Short-run aggregate supply. Right.

     h.   Aggregate demand. Left.

     i.   Short-run aggregate supply. Left.

3. a. Aggregate demand shifts to the right.

    b. Price level rises and real output rises.

    c. Price level rises and real output stays the same.

    d. No. Over time, people and firms adjust to the new higher amount of spending by raising prices and wages.

4. a. Short-run aggregate supply shifts left.

    b. Prices rise and output falls.

    c. Stagflation.

    d. Shift aggregate demand to the right.

    e. Prices would rise more and remain there.

    f. The high unemployment at the low level of output would put pressure on the wage to fall back to its original value.

    g. No. Increases in the cost of production need to be "accommodated" by government policy in order to permanently raise prices.

5. a. Some firms mistakenly believe that only the price of their product has fallen and they cut back on production. As they realize that all prices are falling, they will increase production at each price, which will shift short-run aggregate supply to the right.

    b. Nominal wage contracts are based on the expectation of a higher price level, therefore the real wage has risen and workers were laid off. As workers and firms recognize the fall in the price level, new contracts will have a lower nominal wage, the real wage falls, and firms increase production at each price level, thus shifting the short-run aggregate supply to the right.

    c. Some firms have not reduced their prices because of menu costs. Their products are relatively more expensive and sales fall. When they realize the lower price level is permanent, they lower their prices and production rises at each price level, thus shifting the short-run aggregate supply to the right.

    d. More slowly from a recession because the adjustment requires that prices and wages be reduced, and they are usually more sticky downward. The adjustment when output is above the natural rate requires that prices and wages rise.

E. Advanced Critical Thinking

1.   Yes. An increase in price expectations shifts the short-run aggregate-supply curve to the left and prices rise.

2.   No. In the long run the increase in unemployment will cause wages and price expectations to fall back to their prior levels.

3.   Yes. If policymakers accommodate the adverse supply shock with an increase in aggregate demand, the price level will rise permanently.

upward, the Phillips curve shifts to the right.

5.   Unemployment returns to the natural rate in the long run, regardless of inflation.

6.   Below, because if prices are higher than expected, more output is produced and more people are employed, thus reducing unemployment.

7.   Aggregate supply shifts left, showing lower output at each price level. Thus the Phillips curve shifts right, showing more unemployment at each rate of inflation.

8.   Less favourable. Now, at each level of unemployment, inflation is higher, or at each rate of inflation, unemployment is higher.

9.   The Bank of Canada is more concerned with low unemployment.

10.   8 percent. Smaller, because people will reduce their price expectations more quickly, shifting the Phillips curve to the left.

D. Practice Problems

1.   a. Shifts short-run Phillips curve to the right.

   b. Shifts short-run Phillips curve to the right.

   c. Move up the short-run Phillips curve.

   d. Move down the short-run Phillips curve.

   e. Long-run Phillips curve shifts left.

2.   a. E

   b. Equal to the natural rate.

   c. D

   d. Up

   e. Right

   f. F

   g. H

   h. Below the natural rate.

3.   a.   Inflation increases, unemployment decreases.

b.   Inflation increases, unemployment stays at the natural rate.

c.   No. Unemployment temporarily decreases, but as people grow to expect the higher inflation, unemployment returns to the natural rate.

d.   Continued attempts to move unemployment below the natural rate simply cause inflation.

4.   a.   Economy moves from A to B because people fail to reduce their price expectations and wage demands, so unemployment rises as inflation falls.

b.   Economy moves from A to C because people reduce their prices and wages proportionately.

c.   Economy moves from A to B because people are unable to actually reduce some of their wages and prices, so unemployment rises as inflation falls.

d.   Case (a), because it is rational for people to distrust a policymaker that has been untruthful before.

E. Advanced Critical Thinking

1.   No one. It was an act of nature.

2.   Worse, because the short-run Phillips curve has shifted to the right.

3.   The economy moves upward along the new short-run Phillips curve. Unemployment will be reduced but inflation will be increased.

4.   The economy moves downward along the new short-run Phillips curve. Inflation will be reduced but unemployment will be increased.

5.   No, the economy faces tradeoffs in the short run. A policy that reduces inflation increases unemployment. A policy that reduces unemployment increases inflation.

CHAPTER 17 Five Debates over Macroeconomic Policy

I. Chapter Overview

A. Context and Purpose

Chapter 17 is the final chapter in the text. It addresses five unresolved issues in macroeconomics, each of which is central to current political debates. The chapter can be studied all at once, or portions of the chapter can be studied in conjunction with prior chapters that deal with the related material.

The purpose of Chapter 17 is to provide both sides of five leading debates over macroeconomic policy. It employs information and tools you have accumulated in your study of this text. This chapter may help you take a position on the issues addressed or, at least, it may help you understand the reasoning of others who have taken a position.

B. Helpful Hints

1. *A policy that destabilizes the economy moves the economy away from the natural rate of output.* Stabilization policy is the use of monetary and fiscal policy to help move the economy toward the natural rate of output. However, if policy lags are long and unpredictable, the economy may have adjusted back to the natural rate of output (from an aggregate-demand or aggregate-supply shock) before the impact of the stabilization policy is felt. In this case, the stabilization policy would then move the economy away from the natural rate of output and the policy would be considered destabilizing.

2. *A political business cycle tends to involve both a monetary expansion prior to an election and a monetary contraction after an election.* Political business cycles are discussed in the text with regard to the policymaker's behaviour prior to elections. That is, prior to an election, a monetary expansion could increase output and decrease unemployment, thus enhancing the probability of the incumbent party's re-election. However, because this will tend to cause inflation after the election, this type of abuse of power usually involves a monetary contraction after the election to reduce inflationary pressures. Thus, the economy would tend to fluctuate between good economic performance prior to an election and poor economic performance after an election.

3. *Most economists support a cyclically balanced budget.* Federal government spending and tax collections depend on the level of output. For example, when output is above the natural rate, Employment Insurance expenditures decrease and tax collections increase, thus moving the budget toward surplus. When output is below the natural rate, Employment Insurance expenditures increase and tax collections decrease, thus moving the budget toward deficit. Inflexible rules requiring a continuously balanced budget would require the government to reduce spending or raise taxes during recessions, and to raise government

spending or cut taxes during economic booms, any of which would destabilize the economy further. Therefore, most economists suggest that the budget be balanced over the course of a business cycle—or what is termed a cyclically balanced budget—as opposed to a budget that is balanced each and every year.

II. Self-Testing Challenges

A. True/False Questions

_____ 1.   Monetary policy affects the economy with a lag but fiscal policy has no lag.

_____ 2.   Monetary policy may suffer from time inconsistency because policymakers have an incentive to engage in a policy that differs from their policy announcements.

_____ 3.   The political business cycle refers to a situation where corporate executives also hold political office.

_____ 4.   Opponents of an independent central bank argue that monetary policy is not an effective tool for influencing voters.

_____ 5.   Supporters of a zero-inflation target for monetary policy argue that the cost of reducing inflation is temporary while the benefits of reducing inflation are permanent.

_____ 6.   Those opposed to a zero-inflation target for monetary policy argue that some of the costs of inflation can be eliminated by inflation-indexed income tax brackets and bonds.

_____ 7.   Government debt tends to redistribute wealth from the current generation to future generations.

_____ 8.   Canada has incurred federal government budget deficits only during wars and recessions.

_____ 9.   Replacing the income tax with a consumption tax may increase saving, but it will tend to benefit the rich more than the poor.

_____ 10.   A reduction in the taxes on interest income will increase saving if the substitution effect from the increase in after-tax interest outweighs the income effect.

B. Multiple-Choice Questions

1. Suppose that the economy is suffering from pessimism on the part of consumers and firms. Which one of the following is an activist stabilization policy that "leans against the wind"?
   a. Policymakers should increase the money supply.
   b. Policymakers should increase taxes.

    c. Policymakers should increase interest rates.

    d. .Policymakers should decrease government spending.

2. Which one of the following would **NOT** be stated by an economist who argues that policymakers **should not** try to stabilize the economy?

    a. The first rule of policymaking should be "do no harm."

    b. Stabilization policy has no effect on the economy in the short run or the long run.

    c. Because forecasting shocks to the economy is difficult, well-intended policy could be destabilizing.

    d. Because stabilization policy affects the economy with a lag, well-intended policy could be destabilizing.

3. Which one of the following terms refers to fluctuations in the economy caused by politicians' manipulation of the economy for the purpose of affecting electoral outcomes?

    a. the substitution effect

    b. the discretionary effect

    c. the political business cycle

    d. the time inconsistency of policy

4. Which one of the following terms refers to the discrepancy between policy announcements and policy actions?

    a. the substitution effect

    b. the discretionary effect

    c. the political business cycle

    d. the time inconsistency of policy

5. Which one of the following statements would **NOT** be made by an economist who argues that monetary policy should be made by an independent central bank?

    a. It eliminates the political business cycle problem.

    b. It leads to a lower rate of inflation in the long run.

    c. It increases accountability for monetary policy choices.

    d. It eliminates the time inconsistency problem.

6. Which one of the following is an example of an activist policy action that further destabilizes the economy?

    a. Firms become pessimistic and the Bank of Canada responds with a reduction in interest rates.

    b. Consumers become pessimistic and fiscal policymakers respond with a reduction in taxes.

    c. Firms become excessively optimistic and the Bank of Canada responds with a reduction in the money supply.

    d. Consumers become pessimistic and fiscal policymakers respond with a reduction in government spending.

7. Which one of the following arguments would **NOT** be made by an economist who supports a zero-inflation target for monetary policy?
    a. Inflation imposes costs on the economy such as shoe leather costs and menu costs.
    b. The cost of reducing inflation to zero is temporary while the benefits are permanent.
    c. The cost of reducing inflation to zero could be reduced if a zero-inflation policy were credible.
    d. When there is zero inflation, people's standard of living is no longer eroded by their incomes failing to increase with inflation.

8. Which one of the following tends to be an effect of government debt?
    a. It tends to redistribute wealth from future generations to the current generation.
    b. It tends to redistribute wealth from the current generation to future generations.
    c. It tends to have no redistributive effects.

9. Which one of the following is **NOT** true with regard to government budget deficits?
    a. Budget deficits reduce national saving.
    b. Budget deficits place some of the burden of current spending on future taxpayers.
    c. Budget deficits are the only way to transfer income across generations of taxpayers.
    d. Budget deficits reduce capital investment, future productivity and, therefore, future incomes.

10. Which one of the following would be perceived by an economist who argues that the central bank should not aim for zero inflation?
    a. Those who lose their jobs often have the most skills and experience.
    b. The cost of reducing inflation is concentrated on those workers who lose their jobs.
    c. The social costs of disinflation are smaller than the economic costs of disinflation.

11. Which one of the following statements would **NOT** be made by an economist who argues that the government **does not** need to balance its budget?
    a. The government debt per person is relatively small compared to a person's lifetime earnings.
    b. Budget deficits increase future growth because they transfer wealth from the present generation to future generations.
    c. If parents save more and leave a larger bequest, there is no intergenerational redistribution of wealth from budget deficits.
    d. Budget deficits will not become an increasing burden as long as the debt does not grow more quickly than a nation's nominal income.